THE
DETAILS
ICONIC MEN'S ACCESSORIES

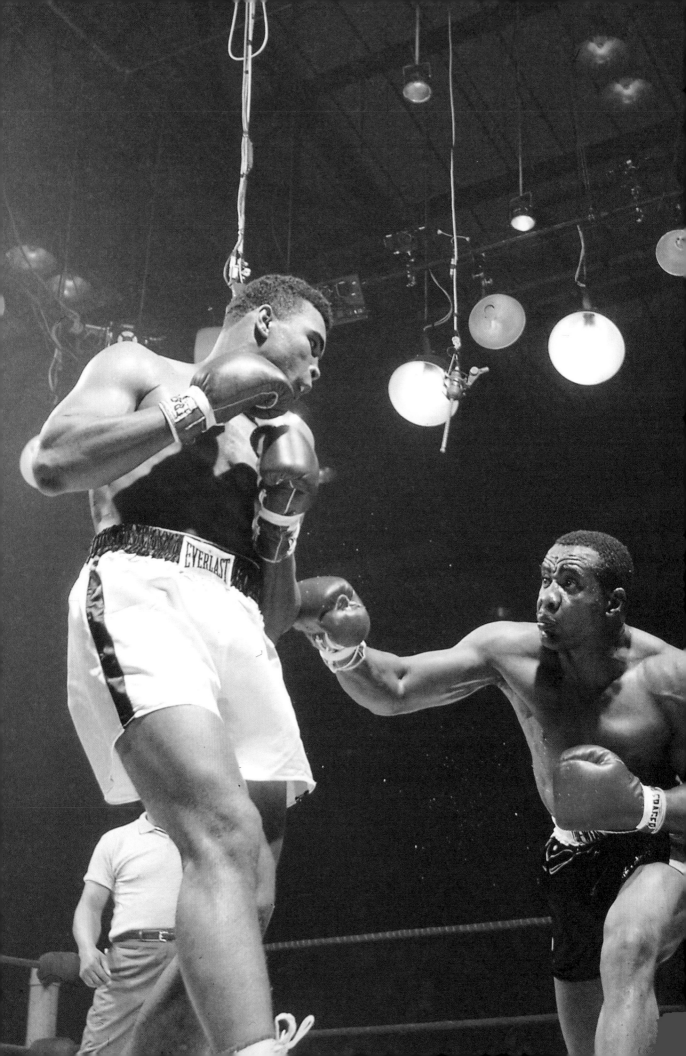

THE
DETAILS
ICONIC MEN'S ACCESSORIES

JOSH SIMS

Published in 2015 by Laurence King Publishing Ltd
361–373 City Road
London EC1V 1LR
United Kingdom

Tel: + 44 20 7841 6900
Fax: + 44 20 7841 6910

e-mail: enquiries@laurenceking.com
www.laurenceking.com

A catalogue record for this book is available from the British Library.

ISBN: 978 1 78067 609 8

Design: Eleanor Ridsdale
Picture Editor: Tom Broadbent
Printed in China

THE DETAILS

INTRODUCTION

Shoes have such metaphoric resonance that the English language, at least, is littered with shoe-related references - to being in someone else's shoes, to the boot being on the other foot, to being well-heeled... Perhaps footwear is of such wide significance because it literally grounds us - our shoes are our point of contact with the earth. Shoes are not merely metaphoric, they are also a distillation of personality. The old fashion adage, said to be passed on from mother to daughter, is that you can always judge a man by his shoes. Battered sneakers? Perhaps not the pillar of the community mother might have wished for. Shiny brogues? Perhaps just a tad boring.

The point, perhaps, is that it is the little things in one's sartorial presentation that make all the difference. It is the details - or 'accessories' as the fashion industry prefers to call them - that give the impression of individuality. A suit is just a suit, however beautifully cut, until it is given character with the right tie or pocket square; a business shirt is typically nothing distinctive until cufflinks make the difference. It is what the seminal London tailor Edward Sexton - who co-founded the revolutionary Nutters on Savile Row in 1969 - calls 'romancing'. Clothes may be the canvas, but the picture is painted with all the details then applied to them.

These are often the smallest of details too - a belt, for example, may only be a humble strip of leather - but are imbued with significance far beyond their size; the buckle might speak a thousand words. What matters is that the choice is personal. If clothes, despite the infinite variety available, are essentially a matter of uniform - and all the more so in those working worlds in which a dress code is enforced, either consciously or through unspoken rules - then one's choice of accoutrements, to give them a more fancy but aptly expressive name, allows the individual to shine through.

The way one wears one's details adds another layer to the self-expression. Frank Sinatra advised that the attitude embodied in wearing a fedora was in the angle of its tilt, Fred Astaire would sometimes wear a tie as a belt, while the Duke of Windsor came up with his own way to tie a knot. Sunglasses in one context - when it's sunny - provide an air of mystery, but in another - indoors, for instance - can make the wearer look like a moron; even the way a pocket square - in itself nothing more than a small patch of fabric - is placed inside a pocket can separate the individual from the rank and file.

Frank Sinatra, wearing his hat at the right attitudinal angle, on the set of *Kings Go Forth* in 1958

It is, however, also very easy to get the details wrong. That many men instinctively seek to show some sign that they are, as Patrick McGoohan put it in TV series *The Prisoner*, 'not a number [but] a person', can lead to rather excessive use of the accessory: the tie isn't distinctive, it's loud; the socks are not original, they're novelty; and so on. Or the details are piled one on another to overwhelming effect. 'Before you leave the house, look in the mirror and remove one accessory', Coco Chanel advised.

She was a woman, of course, and for women the potential to accessorize has, arguably, always been that much greater than it is for men, and perhaps all the more so given that an accessory for a woman is not necessarily expected to have any function other than to look the part. In menswear, a cufflink is chiefly there to fasten your shirt cuffs, braces to hold up your trousers, a bag to carry your stuff in - their expressive qualities are supposedly secondary. And yet the very reverse should be the case: the clothing of men's style is largely unchanging and, compared with womenswear, broadly limited in both scope and imagination. If ever a sex needed accessories to help them stand apart from the crowd, it is the male of the species.

US actor Robert Montgomery in a fetching combination – sweatshirt and silk scarf.

1.
BOOTS

THE BIKER BOOT / THE COWBOY BOOT /
THE WELLINGTON BOOT / THE WORK BOOT

THE BIKER BOOT

The Chippewa Shoe Manufacturing Company was founded in 1901 near the Chippewa Falls, in Wisconsin, USA, from which it took its name. The region was a rugged one, with the logging industry a main employer, and the market for hard-wearing boots seemed to be a clear one. Chippewa, along with fellow boot pioneers Red Wing, would come to define the lasting aesthetic of the American work boot. But it was almost four decades later, in 1937, that the company made perhaps its biggest contribution to footwear history.

Conscious that the various agricultural and industrial businesses across the United States were becoming increasingly corporate, Chippewa spotted the need for a rugged boot that performed in the field but that was also smart enough for professionals and management to wear, or, more specifically, for engineers and land surveyors having to make site visits. The semi-dress, pull-on design was no less rugged than the original boot, but was given much cleaner lines: a 43-centimetre (17-inch) tall, fitted shaft based on an English riding boot, and no laces, these being replaced by chrome or brass buckles at the top of the boot and over the upper at the ankle. The materials and make were upgraded too, using Horween Chromexcel leather and a Goodyear welt construction. Chippewa called it the Original Engineer Boot.

It was not only men with clipboards and hard hats who took to the new style of boot. Other companies were soon producing their own versions, such as that launched by the Portland, Oregon-based West Coast Shoe Company in 1939. In 1941, Red Wing produced its first engineer boot, more aptly named because it saw the style as being for the men who shovelled coal into the engines of steam locomotives, who required a boot to provide protection from the embers that fell out of the firebox and with a side gusset to allow easier movement.

Bikers immediately saw the potential in the engineer boot. The thick black leather could take being splashed with engine oil and other dirt from the

Above: A pair of knee-length biker boots from the US maker Chippewa.
Opposite and below: Marlon Brando on set during the making of *The Wild One* (1953) and in the promotional poster for the same movie.

road, the tall shaft protected the leg from flying debris or the heat of exhaust pipes, and the absence of laces meant there was nothing to get caught up in the machinery. In 1940, Chippewa capitalized on this unexpected market by introducing a new version of its Engineer with bikers in mind: it was shorter, at 28 centimetres (11 inches) tall, which allowed easier pivoting of the ankle for gear changes, and it had a higher heel – actually the heel used for the company's logger boots – which allowed the foot to sit securely on a motorcycle's footrest.

Such was the success of the model that over the next decade the boot quickly became the definitive footwear for bikers. In turn, it also became symbolic of rebellion against the conservative mores of the period, thanks in no small measure to the image of bikers as folk rebels, as cast by the media and the entertainment industry. Marlon Brando wore engineer boots in *The Wild One* (1953), and Peter Fonda a suede version in *Easy Rider* 16 years later. Bikers were already wearing black leather biker jackets – often the classic Perfecto style originally designed by American clothing manufacturer Schott for a Harley-Davidson dealership. The black boots only added to the menace of their appearance.

That, of course, made the style appeal to American youths of the 1950s too, whether they actually owned a motorcycle or not: it was the style that shod the bad-boy cast of *Rebel Without A Cause* (1955), for example. Singer Billy Joel's evocation of teen life of the time, 'Scenes from an Italian Restaurant', refers to 'those days hanging out at the village green, engineer boots, leather jackets, and tight blue jeans'.

Opposite: British comedian Peter Cook in full biker gear, in 1972.
Below: Dennis Hopper, Peter Fonda and Jack Nicholson in a publicity still issued for *Easy Rider* (1969).

THE COWBOY BOOT

Familiar to us from western movies and the country music scene over five decades – whether sported by Clint Eastwood or Hank Williams – cowboy attire has been central to the mythology of American history. The Stetson hat may have appeared most striking on those who could carry it off, but way down below, be they polished and hand-worked or scuffed and dusty, cowboy boots united showman and loner alike. Even if the figure of the cowboy has largely passed into history, to wear part of his style is to seek to recapture a little of the romance he represented: the rugged, manly, pioneer spirit of the upstanding, self-sufficient frontiersman. Figures as disparate as Bruce Springsteen, Ralph Lauren, Steve McQueen, Robert Redford and Paul Newman have all made cowboy boots their own, with the latter continuing to wear off-screen the pair he wore on-screen for *Hud* in 1963.

It was with Hollywood's efforts during the 1930s to turn the mythology of the cowboy into cinematic gold, initially through actors such as Gene Autrey and Roy Rogers, that the cowboy boot was first worn for fashion. Outside America's Midwest, today the cowboy boot can sometimes be perceived as being a largely decorative, folk-art form of bygone dress, with its rococo shape, ornate leatherwork and, of course, more than a hint of the nineteenth century about it, jarring with twenty-first-century urban life. Yet its unisex design – both men and women of the 'Wild West' rode and ranched – was shaped by consideration for its function while riding a horse.

The heel was made high, at 5–8 centimetres (2–3 inches), large and angled towards the instep to help the foot stay in the stirrups but prevent it from passing all the way through them – it also dug into the ground when the cowboy (or girl) wearing the boots had to restrain or pull back on a wayward horse. The toe was made more chiselled so that, when mounting one's horse, it was easier to insert into the stirrups in the first place. The boot's wider opening and lack of lacing not only made it easier to get on while wearing heavy-duty all-weather outerwear but, more importantly, made it easier to free the foot from the boot if the rider was thrown from the horse and the

Opposite: Marilyn Monroe and Clark Gable during shooting of *The Misfits*, 1960.
Above: Among the more understated of cowboy boots, this roper style is from the US bootmakers Justin Boots.
Right: Legendary big screen cowboy Roy Rogers showing off the hand-tooling in his boots and saddle.

boot remained caught in the stirrup. A tight-fitting vamp (upper) kept the boot secure on the foot while upright. The tall shaft afforded the rider's legs protection against stones, brambles and the like (the shorter version of the cowboy boot known as the 'roper' came in with rodeo, since rodeo riders had to be free not only to ride but also to run after and rope a calf). Even the thickness of the leather afforded the foot and lower leg protection from knocking against both stirrups and leathers.

As for the decoration, that was an imaginative response to the fact that cowboy boots are stitched on the outside so that no seams are left to rub against the foot or leg on the inside. The more ornate take on the boot, with inlays and overlays of boldly patterned and coloured leathers, only arrived on later styles of cowboy boot, from the 1920s onwards, when boots began to be worn for show as much as for work. Rodeo blended ranch skills with entertainment, while Hollywood sought to give its big-screen cowboys ever more spectacle.

Hollywood had a lasting effect on the appeal of the cowboy boot, encouraging its embrace as a symbol of American history, of heroic individualism, much as it did with denims. By the 1960s it had become a fashion staple, sometimes in favour, sometimes down on its luck. Sometimes a movie such as *Smokey and the Bandit* (1977) – a modern-day reinterpretation of a western – with a cowboy boot-clad Burt Reynolds, would spark a revival.

Remarkably, given the level of consideration that went into the cowboy boot, exactly who invented them has escaped record. They represented a genuine departure from the Wellington-style boots worn previously, until around 1865 (when the American Civil War ended). It has been suggested that the style probably originated in either Texas or Kansas; certainly one forerunner was Kansas's Hyer Boot Company, established by Charles and Edward Hyer after taking over their German immigrant father William's shoemaking business in 1880. However, ancient cultures in which the horse figured highly also wore comparable footwear. The fifth-century Huns of Central Asia may have passed on their similar boot design to the Moors, who took it to Spain; the Spanish then took it to the New World, in particular Mexico and California, where they became, in effect, the first cowboys – the *vaqueros*.

Right: A cowboy boot in ostrich skin – more decorative than functional – from Tony Lama
Opposite page: A Texan cowboy relaxes on the ranch.

MEMBER
TEXAS & SOUTHWESTERN
CATTLE RAISERS
ASS'N. INC.
POSTED

PITCHFORK
LAND & CATTLE CO

THE WELLINGTON BOOT

Above: Knee-length leather riding boots, with spurs and red lining, formerly belonging to the Duke of Wellington – from whom the rubber boots take their name.
Below: The Russian-American Rubber Manufacturer promises in this advertisement of 1900 that it makes 'The Best Galoshes in the World'.

Arthur Wellesley, the 1st Duke of Wellington – the man who defeated Napoleon at Waterloo in 1815 – would probably have preferred that his fame for posterity did not lie in a rubber boot. In fact, the association between Wellesley and the practical pull-on style beloved of farmers, industrial plant workers, ramblers, fishermen and country folk and festival-goers is a slight one. In 1817 he did request that his shoemakers, Hoby of St James's Street in London, adapt a basic eighteenth-century Hessian boot (the standard military boot of the time) to something more to his liking. This meant it being made in soft, more lustrous, more comfortable calfskin leather ('I am pained by those which I wear at present,' he wrote to his shoemaker), cut closer to the leg – all the better to wear with the newfangled fashion called trousers – and, in one version, extending above the knee, affording some protection in battle for that vulnerable part of a horse-rider's leg. The style caught on, as much with city gentlemen and Regency dandies as with other officers, and, in part thanks to the duke's status as a national hero, remained fashionable until the 1840s. But it was still a long way from being a rubber boot.

It took an American by the name of Hiram Hutchinson to see the potential for footwear in the new vulcanization process developed by Charles Goodyear to give rubber a lasting flexibility. He wanted to use it to make all-rubber boots and then sell them to agricultural labourers in France. In 1853 he bought the patent from Goodyear and launched the Flexible Rubber Company in Montargis, France. The following year, Hutchinson launched his 'À l'Aigle' ('Homage to the Eagle') style, the name perhaps appearing to give a nod to the French imperial eagle, although he had the American eagle more in mind. The new kind of boot offered good grip, comfort and, above all, waterproofing, unlike every aspect of the wooden clog then typically worn by labourers in the French fields. So much in demand was the boot that by 1857 the company (later renamed Aigle) was making 14,000 pairs a day.

Nor was Hutchinson the only entrepreneur to see money in rubber footwear. Another American, Henry Lee Norris, thought that Scotland, with its notoriously wet weather, would be a good location for another rubber boot company. His North British Rubber Company, as he named it, launched in 1856. It was this company that introduced the idea of a Wellington boot coloured something other than black, and launched a green rubber boot specifically to appeal to landowners and gamekeepers. Despite the basic qualities of their products – both left and right boots were typically made on the same last, for example – both businesses did well. Their success was sealed by the outbreak of World War I, with the blood and endless mud of trench warfare requiring the supply of well over a million pairs of rubber boots, or 'wellies' as they became known (while being called gum-boots or rain-boots in the United States).

After the war, production also began in Russia, with Stalin ordering the building of some 17 factories across the Soviet Union. Such was the state's enthusiasm for honouring the worker that, in the early 1960s, the utilitarian nature of the rubber boot saw it being hailed as a form of 'socialism style', while the leather boots Russians had worn for centuries were suddenly decried as 'capitalism style', to the point that leather footwear all but vanished from shops across the USSR. In contrast, despite the rubber boot's basic functionality, in the UK the style rapidly attained an image more closely associated with the upper classes (of which Wellington had been very much a part). The so-called 'green welly brigade', comprising those wealthy and leisured enough to participate in country pursuits such as shooting, riding and fox hunting, would team their Wellington boots with their waxed jackets.

Above: Water- and mud-proof, the Wellington is perfect for life on a farm – as shown here by a Sicilian lemon plantation worker in 1969.

THE WORK BOOT

The boot is in many respects the grandaddy of men's footwear. Indeed, it was only from the post-World War I years that most men would have considered wearing shoes rather than boots. The protection afforded by the boot – and the fact that most men who could afford to do so rode a horse, or walked long distances if they could not – meant that footwear that did not cover at least the ankle was impractical. Even today, many styles of boot nod to those equestrian beginnings, the jodhpur boot and chukka boot among them – the latter, as the name suggests, having its origins in the sport of polo. Boots probably originated around 1000 BC among the nomadic, horse-based societies of eastern Asia, who combined shoes and leather leggings into one item, and were later carried by the Mongols to China, India and Russia.

In late eighteenth-century Europe, men started to wear knee-high riding boots even when not riding, such was their utility. The celebrated English dandy Richard Nash had a habit of confronting men in the street and pointing out: 'Sir, you have forgotten your horse!' Conversely, for the early nineteenth-century dandy George 'Beau' Brummell, so important was the lustre of the leather of his boots that he is said to have had them polished with champagne. Indeed, that boots were the dominant form of men's footwear is perhaps suggested by the numerous references to them in idiomatic English: to put the boot in, to die with one's boots on, to pull oneself up by one's boot straps, to be as tough as old boots, and so on.

After the 1920s, however, as the shoe became equated with smartness, few forms of ankle-length boots remained suitable for daywear. The elastic-sided Chelsea boot of the 1960s was an exception, with the Anello & Davide-designed Beatle boot variant, created for the band, assisting in giving the style a minor resurgence. Most boots of the twentieth century, however, had functionality to the fore. Boots were for farmers, miners and factory workers to work in, or for soldiers to march in (military style having been the key influence on the 'fashion' boot and, to a large degree, on menswear generally, since the seventeenth century). In Europe, the bench-made hobnailed boot – in which stubby nails were fixed into the sole to enhance its durability – became the commonplace footwear of the labourer, while in the United States softer-soled work-boot styles were introduced by such companies as Chippewa and Red Wing. The latter was established in 1905 in Minnesota and found a ready market for its Brown Chief and Irish Setter styles among those working in the region's forests and iron mines.

If the shoe evolved to meet the demands of fashion, it was the need to meet certain environmental conditions that prompted the creation of what would become staple boot styles. The Munson boot, for example, was designed by Major Edward Munson of the US Army medical department following research he began in 1912 to create a boot that combated problems faced by soldiers in the field. Having measured the feet of some 2,000 servicemen over four years, he created a distinctive, spoon-like toe shape that prevented the boot from putting pressure on the toes. This shape would become the standard for many national armies, as well as being taken up by makers of general-purpose work boots.

War also inspired the creation of the crepe-soled, suede desert boot. Variations of this had been worn in rough form by the traders of Cairo's Old Bazaar for centuries, when Nathan Clark, of Britain's C. & J. Clark shoe-making family, spotted British officers also adopting the boot for its comfort when worn in the hot sands. He took the idea back home and in 1949 had pattern cutter Bill Tuxhill create an updated version, which many at the company were convinced would never sell. They were very wrong.

Above: A soldier of the Democratic Republic of the Congo's military, in a lull between fighting rebel forces in 2012.
Below: Anthony Minerich and Vincent Kemenovich, Pennsylvania coal miners, 1927.

Above: James Dean in Indiana in 1955, on his uncle
Marcus Winslow's pig farm.

Singer George Michael
of Wham! relaxes
in loafers and 'Club
Tropicana' style in 1985.

2.
SHOES

THE LOAFER / THE PLIMSOLL / THE
SLIPPER / THE ESPADRILLE / THE OXFORD
& DERBY

THE LOAFER

In 1987, Prime Minister Brian Mulroney of Canada faced what the newspapers dubbed 'Gucci-gate'. No actual corruption was involved, but the very fact that Mulroney owned some 50 pairs of Gucci loafers was enough to cast him as a politician completely out of touch with ordinary voters. The Gucci loafer had been a statement of success, or of aspiration, for more than 30 years by that point. On opening its first American office, in 1953, the leather-goods company had noticed the huge popularity of the loafer there, so decided to create its own, more Italianate version. It streamlined it with an almond-shaped toe, added a snaffle bit across the upper – a nod to the company's saddle-making heritage – made it in fine calfskin and, perhaps most crucially, offered it in black.

Until that point the loafer was a style of shoe available principally in brown – defining it, in an age when correct business attire still insisted on black shoes, as a quintessentially casual shoe. With Gucci it was reinvented as formal, chic, proper: a personality only reinforced when such stars as Fred Astaire and Clark Gable started to wear them. By 1962 the shoe had become part of the collection at the Costume Institute of New York's Metropolitan Museum of Art.

Gucci, however, was clearly not the first company to popularize the loafer style. Credit for that might arguably lie with Raymond Lewis Wildsmith, of Wildsmith Shoes in London. In 1926 he was commissioned by King George VI to make a comfortable, lace-free shoe to wear indoors at his country house. Wildsmith complied, effectively creating the first slip-on style of shoe for men. It was subsequently introduced into his own collection and named the 582, later the Model 98.

But it would be another few years before the loafer came to be defined as a recognizable style, and that happened in the United States. Shoes based on the Native American moccasin had long been worn by settlers. In 1930, Norwegian shoemaker Nils Gregoriusson Tveranger, created a loafer style likely influenced by the footwear of the Iroquois tribe, which he discovered

Opposite: Singer Elton John relaxes in his hotel room, in robe and moccasins, 1973.
Above: A classic black penny loafer from Brooks Brothers, the consummate American retailer of preppy style.
Right: Cary Grant, in loafers, poses for a publicity still for *That Touch of Mink* in 1962.

during his teenage years an an apprentice shoemaker in the US. Known as the Aurland moccasin, the shoe also resembled the traditional shoes worn by Scandinavian fishermen. Tveranger exported his shoe to the rest of Europe, from where it inspired the launch of the loafer in the US.

Around 1933 New Hampshire-based company Spaulding began to market a soft, slip-on style of shoe it called the 'loafer', said to be based on the Aurland. Meanwhile an employee of the G. H. Bass shoe company, based in Wilton, Maine, made his own discovery of the traditional Norwegian moccasin while on a trip around the country. In 1936 Bass introduced its version, adding a thick sole in order to make the style sturdier, dressier and more suitable for the American market. He also added what would become the most celebrated aspect of the design: a leather strap across the front with a diamond-shaped cut-out. Bass called the style the Weejun, a corruption of 'Norwegian'.

When, during the 1950s, American college students began wearing the style, they would slide a coin into the slot – be it for good luck or for that emergency phone call – giving the style its nickname: the penny loafer. One company, Kerrybrooke, even produced a model, the Teenright Smoothie, that came complete with the coin. James Dean made loafers part of his style, with denims and white T-shirt; Elvis Presley wore a pair in white in *Jailhouse Rock* (1957).

Those pennies, or Gucci's snaffle, were not the only flourish to add distinction to an otherwise streamlined style. In 1952 shoemakers Alden, of Massachusetts, created the tassel loafer. Other decorations followed. Sebago introduced the 'beef-roll', a section of visible stitching on the shoe's toe box that resembles a cut of beef tied up with cooking string. Fringes (known as kiltie fringes) were also popular, as was the so-called Venetian style, with no decoration at all.

The loafer's adoption by Ivy League students ensured that it would enter the menswear canon. Neither too dressed up nor too undressed, and extremely comfortable, the loafer not only signalled one's preppy credentials but also suggested a certain youthfulness. Students wore their loafers literally until they fell apart, sometimes keeping the parts together using duct tape. Late for class, they would throw on their convenient loafers without socks – which would inspire a fashion all of its own, one adopted during his leisure time by John F. Kennedy, both as a young man and when president.

Opposite: Actor Ian Ogilvy is best known as Roger Moore's replacement as 'The Saint'. Here he poses in 1988, a decade after *Return of the Saint*, in quintessential 1980s style – pale socks and loafers.
Below: Michael Jackson performs during the Victory Tour in Los Angeles in 1984 – in signature rumpled socks and black loafers.

THE
PLIMSOLL

The ancestor of what by the 1980s had become the ubiquitous sneaker – or 'trainer' in the UK – was designed for much more sedate purposes: walking on the beach. The original plimsoll was a product of mid- to late nineteenth-century British seaside holidays and the discovery by working men that their sturdy boots were inappropriate for the setting and the sands alike. The result was an uptake of the so-called 'sand shoe' – a new, cheap, lightweight shoe with a cool, fast-drying canvas upper and a rubber sole, popularized by the Liverpool Rubber Company (established in 1861 and later bought by Dunlop). The sole was secured to the canvas by way of a rubber strip that gave the shoe its name, echoing as it did the white 'Plimsoll' line on a ship's hull, introduced in 1876 to indicate the maximum permitted depth of immersion of a ship when loaded with cargo. The seafaring analogy was particularly apt given its typical beach use, even if the stylish and well-to-do of the Victorian era were more likely to wear theirs to walk the promenade rather than actually risk getting them wet.

Advances in the use of rubber also saw variations of the plimsoll developed in the United States. Vulcanization, a process pioneered in the United States by Charles Goodyear (and in Britain by Thomas Hancock) by which rubber is hardened ('cured') by the addition of sulphur at a high temperature, was first licensed by the Goodyear Metallic Rubber Shoe Company during the 1890s. It was one of nine small rubber companies that in 1892 consolidated to form the US Rubber Company, which by 1913 had created more than 30 different brands of plimsolls. The decision was made to consolidate further with a single canvas and rubber product: the preferred brand name, Peds – from the Latin for foot – was already taken, so three years later they settled on Keds, which launched in 1917.

That was the year that also saw the launch of what would become perhaps the most famous branded plimsoll of all: the Converse All Star basketball shoe, with a distinctive rubber toe-cap to prevent both the big toe wearing through the canvas and damage to the shoe if dragged over the ground during

Opposite: Paul Newman in 1965, wearing a button-down shirt, corduroy trousers and plimsolls.
Below: Arguably the definitive plimsoll, Converse's All Star high top.

Above: Delinquent gang warfare, musical style – a still from the movie version of *West Side Story* in 1961.

some athletic manoeuvre. The style was the creation of the Converse Rubber Shoe Company, founded in 1908 in Malden, Massachusetts, and quickly establishing a reputation as makers of rubber-soled shoes for leisure and, increasingly, for sports use. Plimsolls proved ideal for court sports. Converse had launched a tennis shoe in 1915, for example, and many companies patented new sole patterns affording different kinds of grip or said to protect the playing surface, lawns especially. Yacht sailors also appreciated the plimsoll for its grippiness. Antarctic explorer Robert Scott took pairs of plimsolls as part of the supplies on his first Antarctic expedition, from 1901 to 1904, while the British armed services made them part of standard issue kit for use during PT, or Physical Training. On leaving the services men often kept their plimsolls as a memento.

Converse would later offer its plimsoll as a boot, with company salesman and ex-basketball star Charles 'Chuck' Taylor suggesting the addition of a patch to protect the ankle. The boot, which became the staple of college sports in the US for many subsequent decades, was available only in black until 1947, when a white version was introduced; it then fast became part of the uniform of the American teenager of the 1950s, along with a white T-shirt and a pair of Levi's. By the mid-1960s, plimsolls in the US were widely referred to as 'sneakers', a word coined by N. W. Ayer & Son advertising man Henry McKinney, for the soundless steps that wearing them allowed. By 1966 the Converse take on plimsolls had become the firm market leader and the company had introduced seven colour options. This arguably heralded the advent of the sneaker as a site for bold and bright decoration, especially with the wide availability by then of synthetic materials.

Despite the 1970s onwards seeing sports shoes increasingly designed specifically for individual sports, together with some outlandish styling, fashion remained fond of the minimalistic simplicity of the plimsoll and the way that, like denim, it improved aesthetically with age. Plimsolls formed a stylistic component of key, typically music-led subcultures from the late 70s onwards, too, including American punk rock, grunge, American West Coast hip hop, hardcore punk and EMO, as well as many other fashions with a retro leaning.

Right: The hard rock group AC/DC in 1990, with guitarist Angus Young in trademark plimsolls and school uniform.

THE SLIPPERS

A pair of slippers, for those who wear them, is like an old friend. While other clothes are abandoned and replaced as they grow tired and frayed, slippers are loved even more for being battered, for having been moulded to one's own feet over daily use. Slippers or house shoes represent, perhaps, a break with the working day: they are symbolic of seclusion within the domestic sphere, where comfort rules over propriety. They hail from the East, like the pyjamas that are sometimes worn with them: one story has it that slippers originated within the harems of the great sultans, where concubines and slaves were deliberately shod in these relaxed but backless and insubstantial shoes so as to make attempted escape through the rocky desert an even more unappealing notion.

As befitting their Eastern heritage – although almost every ancient culture has some variation of the style – slippers also made it much easier to sit cross-legged without removing one's footwear and even minimized damage to one's expensive Persian rugs. Like pyjamas too, slippers would, by the late twentieth century, come to be regarded as somewhat lacking in sex appeal, and would be associated more with the elderly. In English vernacular the expression 'pipe and slippers' came to suggest the staid, conservative and unadventurous.

And yet this ancient style of footwear also has a younger, dressier counterpart. Although the style existed before it received a royal makeover, in the mid-nineteenth century Prince Albert, husband of Queen Victoria, commissioned what would become the definitive version: a quilting-lined, velvet-uppered, thin-soled and low-heeled shoe (with a back), which was never intended to be worn outside – despite what, much later, fashion from the 1980s onwards would suggest. Indeed, the Albert slipper, or sovereign dress slipper, allowed gentlemen of the period to be comfortable around the house and in informal company, without bringing detritus into the home from what were then rudimentary roads.

The slipper, which might be embroidered with a crest or monogram on the upper, or decorated with a grosgrain bow, would be worn with one's otherwise unchanged everyday dress. At a time when dressing formally for dinner was still the respectable thing to do among the upper classes – an etiquette observed until as late as the 1930s – slippers might even be worn with dinner dress if one was entertaining at home. A gentleman might keep a second pair at his club. The dress slipper came to be a byword for slightly decadent elegance. As an editorial in a 1939 edition of *Esquire* noted, the 'blue velvet formal house slipper with gold monogram' pictured was of the kind being 'worn by well-dressed men at house parties in Palm Beach and other Southern resorts'. The style came to be one of the sartorial signatures of the wealthy bachelor or gentleman rogue: David Niven's debonaire jewel thief in *The Pink Panther* (1963) wears a pair with his red velvet smoking jacket.

The idea of such a smart slipper was largely ignored outside of aristocratic circles until the 1940s, when the new aristocracy – Hollywood stars and the political elite – embraced the idea. Clark Gable was said to wear his dress slippers at home with coloured socks and a carefully colour-coordinated shirt; Douglas Fairbanks Jr was a fan; Senator Robert Kennedy – of a WASPish, well-to-do family of course – wore them with khakis and an old sweater; and actor Peter Lawford, a member of the famous 'Rat Pack', posed for candid shots with his wife and infant son at home in a black pair, worn with a dark suit. Fellow Rat Packer Dean Martin was perhaps one of the first men to make a point of wearing them outside of the home: he occasionally slipped a pair on, with full black tie, to present and perform in *The Dean Martin Show* from the mid-1960s to mid-1970s. The desire to be comfortable, it seems, is a hard thing to leave at home.

Opposite: Jean-Paul Belmondo, relaxing on set – in his slippers – in 1966.
Above: John Lobb, makers of some of the world's finest men's shoes, also turn their hand to slippers.
Below: Actor Mickey Rourke wears velvet slippers to a party in London, 2009.

THE ESPADRILLE

The espadrille, or alpargata, has strong associations with fine dressing on fine summer days: it is part of the nautical style of the French Riviera during the 1920s, and, teamed with a pastel suit with rolled sleeves, of the tropical style of the *Miami Vice* TV series of the late 1980s. And high fashion long ago embraced the shoe for women - Rita Hayworth and Lauren Bacall brought them to attention by wearing a pair in *The Lady from Shanghai* (1947) and *Key Largo* (1948) respectively, while in 1970 Yves Saint Laurent introduced a pair with a small wedge heel. And yet this quintessentially Pyrennean style of unisex shoe has not only been made in some form by and for fishermen probably for centuries, but was first produced in any great number in the thirteenth century as a working shoe to be worn by soldiers, specifically the infantry of the King of Aragon.

In the nineteenth century espadrilles were being made for the military of the Catalan-Aragon area, and perhaps more surprisingly, for mine workers, for whom a thin rubber sole might be added to the shoe to help grip in wet conditions. Espadrilles are made by an *alpargatero*, traditionally a man, who sews the soles from rolls of jute rope or braided hemp (the name itself derives from *esparto*, or the Catalan *espartenya*, a kind of grass once burned and then braided to make the soles), to which a seamstress then stitches a linen upper. These uppers are traditionally in black or left in the natural colour of the linen; peasant wearers would keep two pairs, saving the lighter-coloured pair for Sunday best. Ribbons in black might be added to better secure the shoe to the foot by tying around the ankle.

While the espadrille offered little protection for the feet - whether in combat or down a mine - they were extremely comfortable, the soles moulding themselves to the feet and the upper allowing the foot to breathe, an important consideration given the hot summer climate of the region. A pair may have lasted only a couple of weeks, especially in such harsh working conditions, but they were plentiful and cheap: during the Spanish Civil War, when much production was nationalized, soldiers would be issued with two or three pairs each rather than a single pair of leather boots. Moreover, certainly counting for something, they were also traditional. Indeed, Catalonia's national dance, the *sardana*, is performed wearing white espadrilles. By the early twentieth century there were a number of factories in northern Spain, and across the Pyrenees in France, employing thousands of workers - many of them young women, the *hironselles*, who travelled from other parts of the country to work on production through the summer months.

What made the espadrille useful to workers in hot climates also made it appeal to the wealthy on holiday. Pablo Picasso and Salvador Dalí, both Spaniards of course, wore them for their seaside trips, the latter always wearing them in white and from the makers Castaner, while Ernest Hemingway wore them during his prolonged visits to Spain. In the United States, John F. Kennedy would team them with a pair of khakis while sailing his yacht off Cape Cod, while Humphrey Bogart - picking up the idea from his wife Lauren Bacall perhaps - and even big John Wayne were photographed in them.

Below: An advertisement for Carigou liqueur - featuring a romanticized vision of a Catalan musician, complete with beret and espadrilles.
Opposite: A young John F. Kennedy with his sisters Eunice and Patricia at a pool party at the American Embassy in London in 1938.

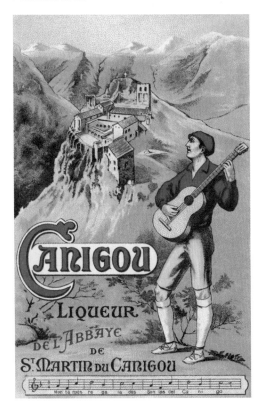

THE OXFORD & DERBY

The Oxford shoe is the most formal of styles, characterized by its clean lines. The look is achieved by stitching the eyelet tabs under the vamp, the main body of the shoe, to give the impression of one seamless piece of leather (in contrast, the less formal Derby, or Blucher, shoe's eyelet tabs are open flaps, resembling a pair of wings). Despite the Oxford's formality, its origins lie in the pursuit of comfort.

It may be apocryphal, but legend has it that around 1825 students at Oxford University, rebelling against the typical habit of most men to wear some form of pull-on boot, which was often so tightly fitted that they found it restrictive, began to cut slits in the side of their footwear. Over time the slits migrated to the front (to become the traditional site of lacing), while the sides of the footwear became lower and lower (to create what was sometimes referred to as a 'half boot') until the ankle was exposed. And thus the modern conception of the shoe – the Oxonian shoe, as it was then called – was set in motion, and the boot began its slow sidelining towards specialist use, notably labouring and horse-riding.

In 1846 *The New Monthly Magazine* quoted a British shoemaker, Joseph Sparkes Hall (to whom the invention of the Chelsea boot is often attributed, so a man with his eye on new styles of footwear), as noting that 'the Oxonian shoe is best for walking', and that the said style, identified by its low cut and three- or four-hole lacing up the front, was now commonly known as the Oxford. In fact, Oxfords have also long been known as Balmorals, especially in the United States, after Balmoral Castle in Scotland, indicating the style's possible Scottish origins. To confuse matters further, in France they are known as Richelieus, after the famous French cardinal and statesman.

The Derby shoe might be somewhat older. Records first mention it in 1872: the style is described in *St Crispin's Magazine* (Saint Crispin being the patron saint of shoemakers) as a 'new tie shoe better than the Oxonian as the seam is not near the tender part of the foot' (i.e. right across the instep); some have suggested that it may perhaps be connected to the 14th Earl of Derby, or even to one of his ancestors. Either way, the ease of the lacing style was adopted by boot makers, most notably following the innovation of a late eighteenth-century Prussian army officer named Gebhard Leberecht Von Blücher, who had standard-issue army boots redesigned with a Derby-style lace opening on the instep to make them easier to pull on and off, and adjustable once on for a better fit. The style of the boot consequently took his name.

Opposite: Peter O'Toole poses for a photograph in a pair of Derbys in 1962.
Below: Cap-toe Oxfords from John Lobb.

Back in civilian life, it would be the turn of the twentieth century before either Oxfords or Derbys would be considered as daywear for the majority of men; before this most men would have continued to wear some kind of boot. Part of the shoe's appeal was undoubtedly the many varieties of detailing it afforded. While Oxfords traditionally came with a toe-cap, variants included, for example, whole-cuts, in which the shoe is made of a single piece of leather, seamed only at the back; and the saddle shoes of the 1940s and 1950s. Saddle shoes were a design actually originating in 1906 from the American sports equipment manufacturer A. G. Spalding, which created it originally for wear during indoor sports. With this casual style the lacing flaps are made of a contrasting colour of leather to the main body of the shoe (creating the look of the shoe wearing a saddle).

Both Oxfords and Derbys found popularity in the form of 'bucks', originally made of buckskin but later in white suede; or with an apron front, in which a separate leather tongue or apron of leather is sewn over the front of the shoe; or with a moc toe, in which the apron design is simulated through stitching alone; and, perhaps most popularly, as brogues. These, with their characteristic decorative perforations and serrated or 'gimped' edging, have their roots in the somewhat makeshift, heel-less shoes of sixteenth-century Irish and Scottish agricultural workers, which were perforated to better allow water to drain through on boggy land. *Brog* means 'shoe' in Gaelic.

Brogues would develop their own variants too, including the wingtip, in which the brogue toe design is extended like wings along the side of the shoe, and the two-tone co-respondent, or spectator, shoe, in which part of the vamp is made of a contrasting colour and fabric, typically white canvas. This was said to be a derivative of the first cricket shoe, created by London shoemakers John Lobb in 1868 to give improved ventilation to players' feet. The style, redolent of the jazz age, may have been inspired by the wearing of spats, or designed so that the darker part of the shoe was protected from dirt or grass stains while allowing most of the shoe to effect a more summery look. It was a favourite of dancers such as Fred Astaire and Gene Kelly, the flashes of white serving to express the skill of their fancy footwork. That the influential Prince of Wales, later the Duke of Windsor, favoured the shoe was enough to make it part of the menswear canon and see it taken up as a staple of Ivy League style.

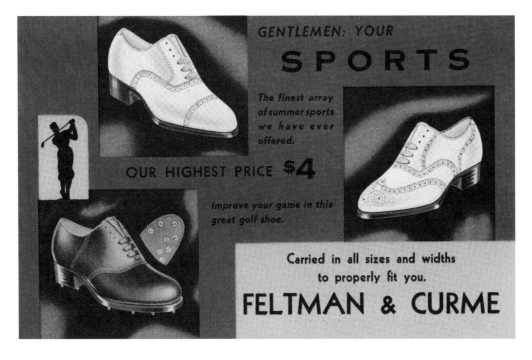

Opposite: A 1936 advertisement for US shoe retailer
Feltman & Curme, featuring some of their most popular
'sports' styles.
Above: Fred Astaire dancing – as he often did – in full
black tie and patent Oxford shoes.

3.
FORMAL HEADWEAR

THE PORK PIE HAT / THE BOWLER HAT /
THE PANAMA & BOATER / THE TRILBY &
FEDORA

THE PORK PIE HAT

Apart from his bullish attitude, the one thing that makes Popeye Doyle stand out – he is the detective played by Gene Hackman in *The French Connection* (1971) – is his hat. Like a fedora, but with the crown flattened down, creased all the way around, and with an upturned, shorter brim – so short it was sometimes called a 'stingy brim' – it resembles that very British savoury confection, the pork pie, devised by bakers around 1760 for fox hunters who needed a form of food on the go. It is from this that the hat takes its name. And although the style is often considered quintessentially American – the headwear of cool jazz types, in particular – and the name was part of the vernacular in the United States by the early 1930s, its origins lie in the same land as those of the pie itself.

The pork pie hat was first popular in Britain during the 1830s, as a hat worn predominantly by women. It did not resurface until mod revival and the rise of ska during the 1970s, the hat winning a brief new popularity with these style tribes thanks to such bands as Madness and others on Jerry Dammers's 2 Tone record label, including his own, the Specials. But even these bands – like the later acid jazz style of the 1980s, which also adopted the hat – took their style influence from abroad, rather than from their own national history. They looked to the original ska heroes (and the rude boy subculture) of 1960s Jamaica, such as Derrick Harriott and Prince Buster, who also favoured the pork pie hat. And their influence in turn? The jazz men of 1950s America.

Certainly the pork pie hat may not have been created in the US, but its identity as the most everyman style among formal headwear was forged there. The pork pie was in fashion as early as the 1900s – at least among young men living in metropolitan centres such as New York – but got its big break when Buster Keaton, the comic star of the silent movies of the 1920s, adopted it as his sartorial trademark. 'In those days almost every comedian you saw affected a derby hat,' Keaton once recalled. 'So I decided to get a hat that was my very own. I knew straw was too fragile for my kind of antics, so I chose felt and designed this particular pork pie.'

Keaton made many hats himself by cutting down and hot-ironing a Stetson or grey fedora, stiffening the brim with warm sugar-water. Since many of his stunts involved water, which destroyed the felt, he would often get through six or more hats while shooting a movie, while others would be snatched off his head by souvenir hunters. Later diverse fans of the style did not tend to have this trouble, including as they did architect Frank Lloyd Wright, pioneer of the atom bomb Robert Oppenheimer, singers Frank Sinatra and Dean Martin, and black activist Malcolm X.

But it was with the hipster jazz men that the pork pie attained a certain urban edge. Dexter Gordon, Wardell Gray, Billy Eckstine, Duke Ellington and, perhaps most famously, Lester Young were among the avant-garde musicians of the 1950s who adopted the style; Charles Mingus even called his 1959 elegy to Young 'Goodbye Pork Pie Hat'. Young, in fact, would appear in magazines of the period under such headlines as 'How to Make a Pork Pie Hat: Jazz sophisticate Lester Young shows how he fashions slick style popular with "hepcats"'. 'Young makes his own pork pies, converting them from ordinary wide-brimmed black hats,' the article explains.

The pork pie's edge was one that would be revisited by American style and pop culture over the following decades, from Ivy League fashion of the early 1960s, through Robert de Niro as Johnny in *Mean Streets* (1973) and Bryan Cranston as Walter White in the hit TV drama series *Breaking Bad* (2008–13).

Above: A pork pie hat from Kangol, one of the more popular makers.
Below: Legendary ska pioneer Prince Buster, in his trademark hat, in 1964.

Above: Gene Hackman as Popeye Doyle, complete with signature pork pie hat, posing for a promotional shot for *French Connection II* (1975).

THE BOWLER HAT

Opposite: Henri Cartier-Bresson's image of a bowler-hatted man who suddenly turned around to face him, on the Allée du Prado in Marseille, 1932.
Above: English men in bowler hats in 1967, when the style epitomized a certain upper-class style.

Not all accessories in the male wardrobe survive changing tastes and needs over the years. Some, however, though rarely worn, remain potent symbols of a certain era, style or even place. Take the bowler hat, for example, which was the essential headgear of the gentleman who worked in London's 'square mile' – financial district – up until the 1960s, symbolic not only of a profession (banking), but also of a class.

When in 1966 the satirical British television show *The Frost Report* featured a sketch on social hierarchies, the working-class figure played by Ronnie Corbett wore a flat cap, the middle-class Ronnie Barker wore a derby hat, and the upper-class John Cleese wore a bowler (he would wear it again for Monty Python's 'Ministry of Silly Walks' sketch). Patrick Macnee's John Steed, the gentleman adventurer of the 1960s series *The Avengers*, was similarly topped off. The bowler hat is the traditional headgear for dressage riders; and the men of the British royal family have worn it occasionally since the 1920s, notably for the annual Cavalry Old Comrades Association Annual Parade in London's Hyde Park, as have members of the imperial royal family of Japan.

More peculiarly, and in more deadly fashion, a bowler hat is also favoured by Oddjob, a villain in the James Bond book and movie *Goldfinger* (1959 and 1964 respectively), who uses a razor-edged bowler hat as a lethal weapon. Indeed, the bowler hat seems to have appealed to many oddball characters in fiction, from Hergé's Tintin sidekicks the Thompson Twins, to *Batman* villain the Riddler, to the hooligan protagonists of Stanley Kubrick's *A Clockwork Orange* (1971), known as the droogs.

Despite its upper-class connotations, the original bowler, a hard felt hat with a rounded, shellac resin-treated crown and a narrow rolled brim, was devised to be worn as a protective item by decidedly working-class men. Created in 1849 by London hatters Lock & Co., the bowler was commissioned by Edward Coke, a younger brother of the 2nd Earl of Leicester, for wear by the gamekeepers on the family's Norfolk estate. Apparently top hats – another style more typically yet not always correctly associated with toffs – were all too easily knocked off and damaged. Coke, who paid 12 shillings for the first bowler, is said to have stamped on its crown to check its robustness before accepting the new design. It was initially better known as a Coke hat, and only in time took the name of the Lock & Co. hatters who created it, Thomas and William Bowler.

For the second half of the nineteenth century it was working men who took on the bowler hat as a functional item of headwear, from hackney cab drivers to street traders and even, because it was an early form of hard hat, shipyard workers. Belfast's Orangemen embraced the style as part of their traditional dress in their annual parades. That it was a working man's hat was reflected in its adoption by the down-at-heel everyman characters created by Laurel and Hardy, Charlie Chaplin (as the Little Tramp) and, later, the American comedian Lou Costello (whose bowler was comedically undersized). Costello's wearing it also followed the tradition of vaudevillians and music-hall performers of donning the bowler, as Laurence Olivier did in *The Entertainer* (1960).

The style was notably successful in the United States, where it became fashionable in the 1890s. It was the choice of real outlaws Robert Parker and Harry Longabaugh, better known in Wild West legend as Butch Cassidy and the Sundance Kid. In fact, a bowler might well have been for many a more likely choice than the cowboy hat portrayed in Hollywood westerns. The hat style perhaps started to win more distinguished associations when it began to be worn as a symbol of authority by the foremen on building sites. Intriguingly, it came to symbolize something very different in Bolivia. There, following the introduction of the hat by British railway workers during the 1920s, it was adopted by women of the Quechua and Aymara peoples, who regard it as a symbol of fertility.

THE PANAMA & BOATER

Some say that the best assessment of quality is to count the number of vueltas – the concentric circles running down the crown; others that the number of weaves per inch, of which there may be up to 2,000, is the best measure. Either way, there is no escaping the fact that the panama hat is, at its best, perhaps the most laboriously hand-crafted of hats. The traditional method of weaving it, with the fibres of the *Carludovica palmata* palm stripped into strands not much thicker than thread, results in a supremely functional style: surprisingly tough, lightweight and extremely breathable. The finest panama hat is the result of perhaps six months' work by a single weaver. Ironically perhaps, overcast days are preferred, since this makes spotting the subtle differences in the colour of the straw strands much easier, while the increased air humidity can also help keep the straw supple.

Just why South Americans have long used this natural material for hats is apparent come any hot weather. Such a use actually dates to the sixteenth-century Incas: although the style of hat they wore was much less structured, it was they who discovered that the native palm leaves could be woven and the resulting 'fabric' pummelled, washed in rainwater and ironed to give it suppleness and shape, each stage a craft in its own right. Later the naturally cream-coloured straw would also be bleached with sulphur from the region's volcanic sources.

The name, however, is misleading: the panama hat, a kind of straw fedora, actually finds its origins in Ecuador, where it is known as the *sombrero de paja toquilla*, and where the centres of manufacturing excellence have traditionally been the towns of Montecristi and Pilé. It took the name when the style first left Ecuador and became international, thanks to the workers building the Panama shipping canal donning them as protection against the sun. Soon the chief hat-production regions of Ecuador, Azuay and Canar had established a vibrant export business, so that even the plants used to make the hats came to be known as panama-hat palms.

It was one Francisco Delgado in the early 1700s who created the first style that would be recognizable as a panama hat of the kind favoured by twentieth-century fans such as Salvador Dalí, F. D. Roosevelt and Frank Sinatra. In fact, the style failed to attain much popularity in Europe until

Opposite: Terry O'Neill's shot of Irish actor Peter O'Toole, in a straw boater, around 1970.

the Exposition Universelle in Paris in 1855, when one of the panama hats brought over for the event was presented to Emperor Napoleon III. In Britain, when Queen Victoria died in 1901 panama hats were worn with the addition of a black band – a mark of respect that became a tradition for the style.

Well-to-do British schoolchildren of the Victorian period would also have worn their own style of straw hat, namely the boater. But this more roughly made, flat-brimmed, flat-topped, broad-banded hat – plaited from a stiffer, 'sennit' straw – had rather grittier origins than might be suggested by its period associations with school uniform, or, indeed, with upper-class Cambridge or Oxford University students punting along the river. The boater was issued to Royal Navy midshipmen in the nineteenth century (also to sailors of the French Navy) to protect them from the tropical sun; back home in grey Britain it became central to the public's conception of the 'old tar' or 'salty sea dog', tanned and tattooed from his exotic travels. Fishmongers, butchers and costermongers of London's East End also took to wearing the boater, as did – at the other end of the social scale – those who enjoyed boating or sailing for leisure. As early as 1822 hatters Lloyd on London's Strand was said to offer some 48 different styles of boater.

Throughout the first two decades of the twentieth century the boater would put in an appearance at some unlikely places. It was part of the uniform of the traditional American barbershop quartet and of vaudevillian entertainers, was said to have been part of the unofficial uniform of early FBI agents, and was a style signature of both the silent screen star Harold Lloyd and the French singer and actor of the 1920s and 1930s Maurice Chevalier. And yet it was the style's connotations of privilege that would remain resonant.

Although some private schools had dropped the boater from their uniform when, in the late nineteenth century, orphanages adopted it for theirs, others embraced the style. The pupils of Harrow, one of England's most prestigious private schools, took to boaters. And after World War II the pupils of Eton College, for example, saw an end to their tradition of top hats in favour of the boater. Pupils of neither institution were particularly fond of their hats, which by the 1930s had all but disappeared from everyday wear as softer, more rakish styles such as the fedora and trilby rose to prominence. In fact, once a boy's schooling was over a typical action was the ritualistic burning of his boater.

Left: Actor Geoffrey Rush in the title role in *The Tailor of Panama* (2001).
Opposite: A suitably hatted man waits for celebrations to start at a ceremony at the Panama Canal in March 1954.

THE TRILBY & FEDORA

Has any element in the male wardrobe suffered such a fall from grace as the formal hat? Up until World War II – and as far back as the 1300s, when hat-wearing took off – for a man to be seen in public without a hat on his head was regarded as not just a breach of social etiquette, but as proclaiming himself as somehow outside of society altogether. Even when fashionable wigs were of such considerable proportions that the wearing of a hat was impossible, a man would still carry one. In Charles Dickens's *Great Expectations* (1861), for example, Pip notices that the convict Magwitch was 'a man with no hat'.

New types of hat were a subject of considerable interest. In 1797 one John Hetherington was fined for disturbing the peace on London's Strand. His new headwear, the outrageous 'top hat', had drawn a crowd and caused a minor riot. Hats were also of especial interest to beavers – the use of beaver fur, once the hatter's material of choice, almost drove the animal to extinction. In 1929 the US National Association of Merchant Tailors proclaimed that the well-dressed man required a dozen different styles of hat.

Quite why the widespread wearing of the hat died out during the second half of the twentieth century remains open to theorizing. Some suggest that soldiers, compelled to wear hats during World War II, returned to civilian life with a new dislike of them, now seeing them as expressive of old-world class structures and conformity in a newly egalitarian and more individualistic society. The rise of the car, with its heater and low roof, perhaps made hats less useful.

Others have even blamed John F. Kennedy: the American president, cognizant of the power of his youthful image, hated hats and refused to wear them, in part because he knew his carefully tousled hair chimed with an electorate in which there were two million more women voters than men. Such was his influence that a representative of the American hat-making industry wrote to Kennedy, pleading with him to start wearing a hat. 'You have set a new pattern for youth,' he wrote. 'What may be a personal attitude for you is becoming a must for these young hatless people.' The plea fell on deaf, unshaded ears. And yet, just a decade earlier or less, the hat had been the very symbol of the stylish individual: this was around the time when even the British Olympic team of 1948 wore formal hats as part of their official uniform.

The most popular styles included the homburg, dating to the 1880s, in rabbit felt, with a curve-edged brim, broad band and steep, stiffened crown creased front to back, said to be an update of the traditional German hunting hat favoured by the Kaiser. The homburg itself, however, was popularized by a relative of the Kaiser, Edward VII of Britain, after a trip to the German

Below left: Harrison Ford as Indiana Jones in *Indiana Jones and the Temple of Doom* (1984).
Below right: Robert de Niro in *The Godfather, Part II* (1974).

Above: Humphrey Bogart in signature private eye attire, 1940.
Below right: Robert Redford and Paul Newman in *Butch Cassidy and the Sundance Kid* (1969).

spa town of Bad Homburg and the hat factory there operated by Johann Mockel, to whom he later granted a royal warrant. More readily recognizable styles today are the fedora and its slightly smaller, shorter-brimmed brother the trilby – signature styles for some of Hollywood's biggest movie stars. Humphrey Bogart, Cary Grant, James Cagney, Frank Sinatra et al all wore one or the other. Certainly, few of the covers of Sinatra's classic albums do not show the singer in a fedora.

Both hats were originally products of the 1890s. The fedora was invented around 1882 and named after a woman, the heroine of Victorien Sardou's play *Fédora*; the trilby around 1895 and also named after a woman, the heroine of George du Maurier's novel *Trilby*. Indeed, both styles were initially intended for and worn by women, albeit those ready to assertively challenge gender stereotyping in clothing. The fedora even became a symbol of women's rights activism. Only in the 1920s did the hats become a more-or-less exclusively male choice (and a rare instance of an item from the female wardrobe migrating to the male, and not vice versa). Both styles were popular because of their relatively low profiles, softness and compact proportions.

These attributes helped the styles gradually ease out the popular homburg. The homburg may have been a favourite of Agatha Christie's fictional Belgian detective Hercule Poirot, and in real life of Winston Churchill and British statesman Anthony Eden (Britons often referred to the hat style by the latter's name), but, like the bowler hat it had effectively replaced, it came to be somewhat associated with the older generation. This did not stop politicians, in particular, from preferring it: German chancellor Konrad Adenauer was often seen in his, while Dwight D. Eisenhower wore one in black for his inauguration as American president in 1953.

Yet the homburg, perhaps, could not quite match the fedora's and the trilby's certain 'snap', especially when cocked at just the right angle. Indeed, the trilby was also referred to as a 'snap brim'. 'Cock your hat – angles are attitudes,' Sinatra is said to have opined. These hats' connotations of cool were no doubt enhanced by their becoming the choice of Prohibition-era gangsters – whose faces they conveniently left hidden in shade. It became a style immortalized as dark and masculine, thanks to the film noir of the 1940s, favoured by hard-bitten private eyes, door-stepping newspapermen and Bogart's cynical bar-owner in *Casablanca* (1942). Much later, Steven Spielberg's Indiana Jones movies put their eponymous hero in one, unusually teamed with casual khakis and a leather jacket.

4.
CASUAL HEADWEAR

THE BANDANA / THE BERET /
THE BASEBALL CAP / THE BUCKET HAT /
THE FLAT CAP / THE COWBOY HAT

THE
BANDANA

Since the late twentieth century the bandana has perhaps been most closely associated with various forms of outsider American culture. Hip hop's gangsta fashion saw West Coast rappers borrow the style of the cholos (a sub-group that expressed the Mexican-American empowerment movement of the 1960s and 1970s) and made baggy trousers, oversized shirts worn untucked and unbuttoned, tattoos and bandanas their own. In gang culture proper, a bandana was a means of signifying affiliation: Californian gangs would wear a red or blue paisley bandana poking from their back pockets or even tied around an ankle. Soft rock performers of the 1980s wore them – Guns N' Roses' frontman made a bandana something of a rock style cliché. And the Hell's Angels-style motorcycle outlaw wore the piratical bandana, ideally bearing the Stars and Stripes or the skull and crossbones.

A simple large square of fabric, the bandana has always proved popular for its versatility – as a scarf, mask or neckerchief, as a sling, bandage or temporary bag. In the early nineteenth century, it was commonplace in America and Europe for a soldier going to war to have his personal possessions bundled up in a cotton bandana, in which would be written, printed or embroidered some consoling verse by his sweetheart; it became a tradition on his making it back home to bring a silk bandana for her.

While the bandana has been used in some form or other for many centuries, this worker's favourite has acted as a statement of outsiderness since the 1700s, not least in England, where the Calico Acts of 1700 and 1702 banned the importation and restricted the wearing of cotton textiles, giving those who still chose to wear a bandana a certain rebel cachet. In revolutionary France, the outsized bandana-cum-cravats worn by the dandy nonconformists known as the Incroyables – the 'unbelievables' – became a signal of political subversion.

Similarly in pre-independence America, the bandana was worn as a political message, though more by virtue of what was printed on it. John Hewson,

Opposite: Axl Rose, rock singer with Guns N' Roses, in his trademark bandana, in 1988.
Below left: A portrait of an Acoma man, published in Edward Curtis's 1926 *The North American Indian*.
Below right: Rapper Tupac Shakur at home in Atlanta, bandana in place.

for example, a textile printmaker who operated in contravention of a ban by the colonial British, printed images of George Washington on a bandana as a symbol of allegiance and, after independence in 1776, as a souvenir of the struggle. Some two centuries later, bandanas would be passed to East Germans in celebration of the fall of the Berlin Wall in 1989.

The bandana was co-opted as a medium of propaganda or campaigning throughout the twentieth century in the United States. Dubbed 'little banners', during World War I bandanas were printed to raise funds towards the war effort. They were handed out by celebrities at bond rallies; used to commemorate such events as World's Fairs and the opening of the Panama Canal; and worn to show one's choice of individuals seeking office – 'Win with Ike for President' exhorted one bandana in 1952. They were also worn to express patriotism and to celebrate American cultural figures such as singing cowboy Gene Autry or western star Tom Mix. Indeed, Hollywood's mythologizing of the cowboy figure in movies from the silent era through to the 1960s was largely responsible for the bandana's rise as some kind of fashion item.

In the years before industrialization, bandanas were typically hand-loomed, so were considered both valuable and collectible. More prosaically, bandanas became a means of advertising: circus founder P. T. Barnum, for instance, printed bandanas to promote his 'Greatest Show on Earth'. With mass-manufacture, the bandana's use in advertising was in full force. In 1926 Kellogg's made a 'Goldilocks and the Three Bears' bandana that could be turned into a soft toy. As well as providing the first example of a promotion printed on a T-shirt, *The Wizard of Oz* was heralded on a bandana, as was *Gone With the Wind* (both 1939). And how better to cash in on the Beatles' first tour of the US in 1964 than by making a bandana?

Commercialization saw the bandana reflect allegiance to a new kind of hero too – that of the sporting arena. From the 1930s to as late as the 1980s, a baseball bandana, sometimes known as a 'homer hanky', might be printed to celebrate important victories for such teams as the New York Yankees, the San Francisco Giants and the Minnesota Twins.

Opposite: Hell's Angels bikers, at rest at Miami Beach in 2000.
Above left: Carlos Santana, wearing his bandana pirate-style, at Woodstock in 1994.
Above right: Actor Dennis Hopper in counter-cultural style, in 1971.

THE
BERET

When, in 1960, photographer Alberto Korda took a shot of a little-known revolutionary in Cuba called Che Guevara, he could not have known that the resulting image – known as 'Guerrillero Heroico' – would become truly iconic. The endlessly reproduced photo became one of the most famous images of the twentieth century: an archetype of the implacable fighter, and also, perhaps, of beret-wearing. The caption for what would become Guevara's official photo pointedly notes that on his beret is the star, 'the symbol of the Commandante'. It has also been noted that the rakishly tilted, soft, round, flat, wool felt cap forms a kind of flattened halo over its wearer.

If, in the popular imagination, the beret has been comically stereotyped as the quintessentially French headwear – worn with Breton top and string of onions – then here was an alternative reading: the beret as symbolic of the man outside society, the freedom fighter, the militant, closer perhaps to the French resistance fighters of World War II.

In the wake of Korda's image, the beret became the choice of student radicals, indeed of radicals of all stripes. The American Civil Rights Movement's Black Panther Party, formed in 1966, similarly adopted the beret, specifically in black – a look echoed by political rap groups such as N.W.A. come the 1980s. The black beret was adopted by a black power organization based in Bermuda, named the Black Beret Cadre; and by Chicano activists in America's Southwest, also during the 1960s, known as Black Berets por La Justicia. Black berets were worn by republican fighters in Ireland, and in Spain by the Basque nationalist group ETA. Even the troops of the criminal organization causing problems in *The Man from U.N.C.L.E.* – a US TV series running from 1964 – wore black berets. John Lennon, a radical of sorts, liked to wear a beret too.

The beret, of course, retains this suggestion of militancy because of its strong association with the military, especially tank crews, since the beret meant that headphones could still be worn, and was one style of headwear suitable for getting out through small hatchways. Just about every national

Opposite: The Cuban revolutionary Ernesto 'Che' Guevara, his arm in a sling – his beret became an icon.
Below left: On the protest trail – a young African American with political badges and beret, during the 1960s.
Below right: Field Marshal Sir Bernard Montgomery, 'Monty', the badge of the Parachute Regiment on his beret.

Above: Jazz trumpeter Dizzy Gillespie, in his signature
beret, in New York in 1958.

army has at some point adopted the beret as its standard-issue headwear – even if they have not agreed on how to wear it (most say pulled to the right, the French say to the left) and despite soldiers often complaining about the style's impracticality and the fact that it is too hot in the sun, offers poor protection in the rain, does not fold flat in a pocket, and requires two hands to put on. Yet some of its wearers, including Field Marshal Bernard Montgomery, commander of the Eighth Army during World War II, made it their signature.

Various colours of beret have been used to denote elite regiments, for which it was a point of pride and a source of esprit de corps. The green beret, for example, was reserved for Royal Marine Commando units in the British Army, and in the US Army also for special forces, as John Wayne helped make famous in the movie *The Green Berets* (1968). In 1979 US military chiefs made a ruling (later rescinded) that only US rangers or airborne units could wear the black beret, although the following year airborne troops were given their own maroon beret. In the UK the British Parachute Regiment is dubbed 'the red berets', although their berets are actually maroon.

The beret itself, however, has more peaceful beginnings. As far back as the fifth century BC, the ancient Minoans and Romans wore a beret of sorts. In the seventeenth century berets were produced in the Basque region of northern Spain and southern France, where local people knitted them in wool for wear during harsh winter months. It was the French who would turn the beret into both a national symbol – for some time it was France's official national hat – and an industry: the first factory, Beatex-Laulhère, began production in 1810. A century later, when the style became associated with working men, some 20 factories across France were producing millions of berets, none of them of a militaristic bent.

Neither were all of its famed wearers: before Guevara, the beret had already begun to achieve a kind of cool thanks to its associations not only with the great and the good – from Pablo Picasso, nodding to his Spanish roots, to Ernest Hemingway – but also with the US jazz scene of the late 1940s and 1950s. Dizzy Gillespie and Thelonius Monk, among the most stylish dressers of the scene, both favoured wearing a beret with their sharp tailoring – one reason why the socially self-excluding hipster Beat Generation also liked it. The beret spoke not only of soldiering, but of the arty and bohemian.

Right: Paul McCartney wears the beret, the rest of the Beatles other kinds of typically Gallic styles of headwear, for a publicity shot in 1964.

Above: American baseball manager Joe McCarthy, of the
Boston Red Sox, with player Ted Williams, in 1948.

THE BASEBALL CAP

After jeans, the baseball cap has arguably become menswear's most ubiquitous piece of Americana. Transcending its sporting origins, it has become the headwear for everyman, worn by presidents and boy scouts, by the US Navy and American law enforcement agencies, by astronauts, racing drivers and rappers, and, of course, by baseball team fans. The baseball cap in its modern form dates only to 1958, when the American baseball authorities settled on the single uniform style, as it is still known today: in essence a cotton or wool broadcloth six-section, fitted, domed crown sewn into a peak where a button known as the squatchee sits, with a broad, curved, stitched visor or bill. The shape and the front visor ensure that the cap stays on during a run, the visor also shielding the wearer's eyes from the sun or the stadium lights.

Until that date, baseball players were free to wear whatever headgear they wanted. The very first baseball caps – as adopted by the New York Knickerbockers in April 1849 – were made of straw, but proved so popular with the players that a smarter and longer-lasting version made of merino wool was introduced five years later. First to commercialize the cap was a company called Peck & Snyder, which dubbed its model simply the 'No. 1': this first production baseball cap was identified by a star logo at the button, and was quickly and widely copied. The style introduced by the Brooklyn Excelsiors in 1860, subsequently known as the 'Brooklyn style', perhaps comes closest to defining the first modern incarnation of the cap.

Over the following years there were many variations – from those with an all-round brim to those more akin to a jockey's cap – and many attempts at innovation. In 1895, for example, professional player Jesse Burkett introduced the sensible idea of a baseball cap with a transparent green-tinted bill, giving players eye protection but also full range of vision, but it did not catch on (although for many decades the underside of the visor was traditionally made in green, switching to grey in the 1970s and later black, each an attempt to better counter the sun's glare). And in 1905, the pillbox

Below left: A promotional poster for a movie from 1927, celebrating the life of legendary baseball player Babe Ruth.
Below right: A US-made, traditional all-wool baseball cap from makers Ebbets Field Flannels.

variety of cap, known as the 'Chicago style', was introduced, the crown comprising a flat top and short vertical side, sometimes with horizontal rings. This was not widely worn, except by the Philadelphia Athletics, who attributed a winning streak from 1909 to 1914 to their lucky headgear, and by the Pittsburgh Pirates for a ten-year spell from 1976. Some teams liked to introduce their own variations – two-colour panels, for example, or piping – for the sake of distinctiveness. Others, such as the New York Yankees, Boston Red Sox and St. Louis Cardinals, have made few changes to their caps, seeing them become classics of the genre as a result.

Indeed, the basic design of the baseball cap underwent few minor changes over the twentieth century that actually stuck. In 1901 the Detroit Tigers became the first team to utilize the front of the baseball cap as an ideal spot for their team's emblem, a running orange tiger – an idea that would later be taken up by other organizations, brands and sloganeers of all kinds, although not by the St. Louis Browns, who shunned all logos until 1945. And in 1903, in part in a bid to make their baseball caps seem more premium, the sporting goods company Spalding introduced a cap with a stitched visor – the so-called 'Philadelphia style' – an idea that did catch on, becoming the standard. During the 1940s the use of buckram to make the visor was phased out and replaced with latex rubber, which meant it could be longer.

The cap would grow in stature too. In 1954, New York-based manufacturer New Era, which had been supplying caps to Major League Baseball teams since 1934, introduced its 59Fifty model, essentially a standard cap but with a taller and stiffer crown and, later, made from a breathable acrylic blend. This would become the league's official model.

A relaxation of dress codes during the 1960s saw baseball fans adopt the cap of their team when watching it play: this was the first step of the baseball cap's entry into menswear's mainstream. Wearing a certain cap was a display of loyalty to hometown and community as much as to a particular team, as exemplified by the sympathetic wide uptake of New York team caps outside New York after the World Trade Center terrorist attacks of September 2001.

Adopted by players of many other sports, the baseball cap has a functionality that has seen it also taken up by farmers, truckers (their cap typically incorporating a mesh section at the rear) and labourers, as well as becoming an icon of urban style.

Below left: The gangsta-rap group N.W.A. – each member wearing that rap style staple, the baseball cap.
Below right: Actor Mark Wahlberg, back when he was rapper 'Marky Mark', in 1991.
Opposite: All time great baseball pitcher Leroy Paige, better known as 'Satchel' Paige.

THE BUCKET HAT

Historically the bucket hat, or fisherman's hat, spans an unlikely fan base. On the one hand it came to suggest a certain nerdiness, helping to define a number of characters in American television comedy series, such as the clownish Gilligan in *Gilligan's Island* (from 1964), J. J. in *Good Times* (from 1974), even Lieutenant Colonel Henry Blake in *Mash* (from 1972), whose fisherman's hat came adorned with fishing flies – splashes of colour in the midst of a khaki-clad war. The bucket-style hat was worn in tweed by Peter Sellers as the bumbling Inspector Clouseau, and became a style signature of director Woody Allen. It also proved a hit with singer Bing Crosby and actor Rex Harrison.

Yet, conversely, the bucket hat was perennially perched on the head of rabble-rousing gonzo writer Hunter S. Thompson and his drug-pumped *Fear And Loathing in Las Vegas* character Raoul Duke. It also – before the baseball cap stole its thunder – became a headwear staple for hip hop, with Big Hank Yank, founding member of the Sugar Hill Gang, having worn one in the very first hip hop video (for 'Rapper's Delight' [1979]). DMC, of Run–DMC, sported a classic Kangol bucket hat from the mid-1980s, while a similar red Bermuda Casual Kangol bucket hat barely left the head of LL Cool J. He might well be credited with making the bucket hat a true hip hop staple from 1983 onwards – indeed, rival rapper Kool Moe Dee illustrated their feud on the cover of his *How Ya Like Me Now* album in 1987 by showing the aforementioned red Kangol being run over by a white Jeep. The previous year, Kurtis Blow had worn a bucket hat on the cover of his album *Kingdom Blow*.

Despite the baseball cap's popularity, the bucket hat's appeal to hip hop endured. In the mid-1990s and beyond, MC Solaar, France's biggest rapper export, was wearing his in bright yellow, Wu-Tang Clan's MC Method Man often donned one, while Jay-Z – frequently spotted in Gucci's logo-covered version – also sported his for the video of 'Big Pimpin'. Many other rapping bucket hat devotees followed – in 2011 a frugal LA rapper, Schoolboy Q, noted that 'I don't spend money on nothing, besides my daughter, bucket hats and weed'. The hats also appealed to those whose music was rather different: Alan 'Reni' Wren, drummer for late 1980s 'Madchester' heroes the Stone Roses, for example.

The eminently practical style – foldable, comfortable, rain-protecting, with a low, all-the-way-round brow that shades both the eyes and the back of the neck – has tough roots. The US Navy had a similar style in white canvas as early as 1886, most typically seen with the stiff, stitched brim turned entirely up, and later referred to as a Dixie cup hat after the disposable paper drinking cup to which it bears a passing resemblance. The floppier brim-down version, known as the tembel hat or Rafael hat (after Israeli general Rafael Eitan, who used to wear one), was worn in 1948 by the Israel Defense Forces fighting the Israeli War of Independence. In the 1960s, the style was being worn in the United States by fishermen, proving the ideal headwear for hours spent stationary in all weathers. In wider-brimmed variations (known as bush or boonie hats, because they were worn out in the field, or 'boonies') it was worn by special forces of both the British and US armies.

Above: Darryl 'DMC' McDaniels, of rap group Run–DMC, in 1987.
Left: A local mariner at Rustico Harbour, Prince Edward Island, Canada.
Opposite: Writer and film director Woody Allen, on set, in his signature bucket hat.

THE
FLAT CAP

The flat cap is held in such fond esteem that diverse peoples lay claim to it. Whether in London or the Yorkshire countryside, the idea that the flat cap is something quintessentially of the local working man's history and geography is held strongly. But, being the essential everyman headwear, the flat cap allows for variations in its style, whether it be in spun wool, tweed, cord, linen or even leather, and whether it be known as the scally cap (United States), the cheese-cutter (New Zealand), the sixpence (Norway), the dai (Wales) or the bunnet (Scotland), the golf cap, the icy cap, the driving cap or the cabbie cap. Indeed, its very diversity of names points to the ubiquity of the style.

While variations on the theme can be traced back to the fourteenth century in several countries, it is Great Britain that can probably lay greatest claim to having introduced the simple cap with its soft, round main part and stiff brim. And in drastic fashion: in 1571, the Tudors introduced an act of parliament – aiming to encourage the consumption of domestic wool – mandating that on Sundays, every male over the age of six (with the exception of the nobility) must wear a wool cap or risk a fine. The act was repealed 26 years later, but that was more than long enough for what was, after all, a useful, affordable, easy-to-wear style of hat to become an accepted part of everyday dress, regardless of one's place in society. Arguably, it helped usher in almost four centuries during which society expected every self-respecting man to wear some kind of hat.

Certainly the cloth cap's 'man of the people' quality has held strong in its public image, one underlined in the UK by Reg Smythe's long-running comic-strip character for the *Daily Express*, Andy Capp, a flat-cap-wearing, belligerent, drunken and sometimes lovable working-class layabout. The flat cap was favoured by construction workers of the great building boom of the 1910s to the 1930s, in both the United States and Europe, before the wearing of a hard hat became obligatory. Across the years, it was spotted on cool creatives such as Alain Delon, Paul Newman and Bruce Springsteen, and was made a style signature of heavy metal group AC/DC's frontman Brian Johnson. Yet the flat cap and its variations (such as the six- or eight-panelled baker-boy or newsboy cap) nevertheless attained a kind of classlessness.

For every comic-book burglar or thug in a flat cap (the so-called 'Peaky Blinders', a post-World War I gang operating around Birmingham, UK, may have been so called because of the razor blades they hid in the peak of their flat caps) was a wealthy driver of one of the early open-top cars, since the cap's low peak and wedge-like aerodynamic lines meant it did not fly off at speed. And although come the 1950s the British Labour Party had begun to express concern with what had been dubbed its 'flat-cap image', in the right circles the flat cap would come to be associated as much with conservatism and the country pursuits of the aristocracy and the well-to-do as with the whippet-racing or pigeon-fancying of the miner or labourer on his day off.

In the 1960s and 1970s the flat cap was embraced by a British working-class street culture in the form of skinheads and the Oi! movement, teams wearing army boots, rolled denims, button-down shirts and that other signifier of working-class style, braces. Twenty years later it was a favourite of British indie bands.

In the United States, however, where the flat cap grew in popularity at the turn of the twentieth century, initially as a cap worn by boys, it never attained associations, chic or otherwise, with the working class. Robert Redford may have worn one as a con artist in *The Sting* (1973), but he also wore one as the wealthy Jay Gatsby in *The Great Gatsby* (1974). Worn back-to-front the flat cap became a stylistic trope of hip hop culture – LL Cool J chose to wear one to collect a Grammy in. It also became a favourite of actor Samuel L. Jackson. The American Olympic squad even wore a white flat cap as part of its Ralph Lauren-designed parade uniform in 2008.

Above: A man in Oldham, northern England, in a traditional flat cap, 1977.
Below: A man poses for a photo in his Adidas jacket and Kangol flat cap – worn reversed – in New York in 1986.

Above: James Dean in 1955, on a trip back to his old
school in Fairmont, Indiana.

THE COWBOY HAT

The cowboy hat is so distinctive and its associations so strong that, even in the twenty-first century, it instantly speaks of a time and place: the American Old West. And that was where and when it was invented, albeit initially as something of a joke. John Batterson Stetson – whose surname became a byword for the style of hat he created – was a hatter on a hunting trip with friends when, to pass the time, he demonstrated how he could make a cloth out of fur by wetting, matting, compressing and heating rather than weaving. With it first he made a blanket. But then, as much for his companions' amusement as anything, he made a hat – outsized in its crown and with an unusually large brim, especially in contrast to the variety of typically much neater styles cowpunchers might then wear, from old Civil War caps to top hats.

But the joke turned serious when Stetson discovered that his design was actually supremely fit for purpose. The hat was lightweight and waterproof; it had a crown tall enough to allow the air to circulate; it had a brim wide enough both to shield the eyes and to channel rainwater away from the shoulders; and it was streamlined enough that it would not easily blow off when riding a horse at speed. Wearers soon found other uses too: the brim was useful for fanning a fire, the large capacity of the crown for watering one's horse – although the nickname of the 'ten gallon hat' that it would later gain was purely figurative.

These benefits had all been explored before in hats in other cultures. *Vaqueros*, the cowboys and cattle ranchers of Mexico, had their sombrero, a style said to be a derivation of one brought to the Americas by the Spanish conquistadors – themselves keen horsemen – who in turn took the idea from thirteenth- and fourteenth-century nomadic Mongols. But the first American settlers to travel west had not been above fashioning their own hybrid headwear to give them the all-weather protection they needed; indeed, the expansion west was led by fur trappers supplying the raw materials to meet the high demand of the eighteenth-century European courts.

Opposite: Paul Newman in cowboy hat, posing for publicity shots for the comedy western *Pocket Money* in 1972.
Below left: Silent movie-era actor Roy Stewart, posing with both revolvers ready.
Below right: John Wayne – the king of screen cowboys – tries on his choice of hats.

Above: Actor Larry Hagman, best known for playing 'J.R.' Ewing in the series *Dallas*, in full Texan attire.

It was Stetson, however, who finessed and formalized the cowboy hat with the exaggerated proportions of his version. One story has it that he sold his prototype hat to a passing frontiersman for five dollars, then kept seeing the same man around Philadelphia, prompting him to think there could be a business in making the style. Certainly the big hat was quickly a success when it went into production in 1865.

His 'Boss of the Plains' model, as Stetson called it, with an 11.4-centimetre (4.5-inch) crown and 10-centimetre (4-inch) brim – the 'most popular cowboy hat', as it was advertised – would soon be followed by other variations, each a natural product of their use. Inevitably the crown became creased, so Stetson produced a model with a centre crease, known as a Carlsbad crease after Carlsbad, New Mexico, and arguably the definitive cowboy hat. Holding the hat by the crown often resulted in four dents, so Stetson produced a version with the crown similarly indented, the Montana. Wearers would each know how to 'twist a lid', to give their hat its own personalized shape – and when they returned east, wealthy after their western ventures, they wore a Stetson as a mark of their success.

The style quickly came to indicate the frontier life, even in the already bustling cities of the East Coast. Stetson's styles were worn by figures who would become iconic in Wild West lore – Buffalo Bill Cody (who had an extra-wide-brimmed custom style made), Wyatt Earp, Will Rogers and Tom Mix, as well as Calamity Jane and Annie Oakley. The hat's symbolism gained further currency as a result of Hollywood's retelling of the lives of such figures through the western genre of movie from the 1920s onwards, as well as through stylized singing-cowboy stars such as Roy Rogers, Gene Autry and Hank Williams in the pre-World War II decades. Since the 1970s American fashion giants, including Ralph Lauren, have tapped into a longing for both a national style and a history since overshadowed by urbanization and industrialization.

Below: Montgomery Clift, pensive in his cowboy hat, shot on the location of *The Misfits* (1961).

5.
UNDERWEAR

BOXER SHORTS / BRIEFS / SOCKS /
THE VEST / PYJAMAS / SWIMWEAR

BOXER SHORTS

Boxer shorts had their origin in the boxing ring. Fans of the looser-fit men's underwear – eternal rival to the Y-front or brief – can thank one Jacob Golomb for popularizing the style. In 1910 the sporting goods entrepreneur, then aged just 17, founded the Everlast sportswear company as a maker of swimsuits. A few years later, in 1917, Golomb was introduced to the soon-to-be legendary fighter Jack Dempsey. The boxer asked him to design and make a range of training gear for him, from protective headgear to shorts that would make crucial footwork easier. After Dempsey won the World Heavyweight Championship two years later, Golomb's new lighter, looser, elastic-waisted boxer's shorts – a marked improvement on the leather-belted variety typically worn until then – began to catch on.

Golomb believed in their potential, and in 1926 he founded the Union Underwear company to make the shorts, the design of which he had tweaked to make them more of an everyday item. By the 1930s the wearing of boxer shorts as underwear had became a full-on (though short-lived) fashion craze in the United States, so much so that Golomb also manufactured them under licence with the Fruit of the Loom brand (itself dating to 1871). It would, however, be some years before the boxer short style would become a staple and customers would get over the perceived lack of 'masculine support'.

Certainly boxer shorts became a hit less for their macho boxing associations and more because they were a break with what was available for men's underwear until that time: heavy, hot undergarments, often made of wool and, one might imagine, far from hygienic. Indeed, the boxer short represented a way-station in the evolution of men's underwear towards the ever more lightweight and minimal: boxer shorts were in some sense a cut-down and looser version of long-johns, which in turn were effectively the bottom half of a new two-piece arrangement of the nineteenth-century all-in-one 'union suit'. So freeing were early boxer shorts, in fact, that some also offered the supposed benefit of what was known as a 'balloon seat': a panel of extra fabric in the rear of the shorts that allowed movement without the boxers pulling against the body.

Opposite: American heavyweight boxer Rocky Marciano, in Everlast shorts and Tuf-Wear gloves, in 1951.
Below left: Ryan O'Neal in a Spanish promotional poster for *What's Up, Doc?* (1972).
Below right: Laurel and Hardy, caught with their trousers down again, during the 1920s.

The new boxer shorts – typically then neatly fitted with a French button-back or tie-back arrangement, rather than the later front-snap closure and elasticated-waist styles – also provided sartorial interest in the variety of patterned or shirting fabrics that could be used in their manufacture. Some would even prove a barometer of the times, as witnessed by the popularity of 'atomic' prints in the 1950s and novelty boxer shorts in the late 1980s. One company, Joe Boxer, even faced criminal charges for forgery in 1985 when it made a style printed with $100 bills. It was in the 1980s that boxers, having nudged briefs out of fashion – in large part thanks to Levi's classic 1985 'Launderette' TV advertisement – became the choice of upwardly mobile yuppies. Much earlier, the brightly coloured silk boxer shorts popular in the United States during the early 1930s were said to provide men with an escape from the woes of the Great Depression – offering some hidden colour under their dour exteriors.

It was exposure that really led to the uptake of the boxer short internationally. Older-fashioned styles of underwear were still commonly worn in the US well into the 1930s, and in the UK until 1947, when John Hill of British underwear manufacturer Sunspel travelled to the US and returned with the idea. But boxer shorts were the standard-issue underwear for American troops, and World War II – and the subsequent maintenance of US military bases overseas – did much to transmit the appeal of the style far and wide. Like the T-shirt, which also originated within the armed forces as an item of underwear, GI boxers originally came only in white, and later – after it was determined that white clothing (even underclothing) provided too easy a target for enemy snipers – only in olive drab. GI wartime boxer shorts also reintroduced the outmoded notion of boxer shorts being given a snug fit through the use of ties at the side as, with the requisitioning of rubber and metal for the war effort, even stripping boxer shorts of these materials was deemed a national necessity.

Opposite: Mickey Rooney poses in a still from *Sound Off* (1952).
Above: James Caan in a still from *Slither* (1973).
Right: British boy band Take That pose in boxing-inspired attire in the video for their debut hit, 'Do What U Like', in 1991.

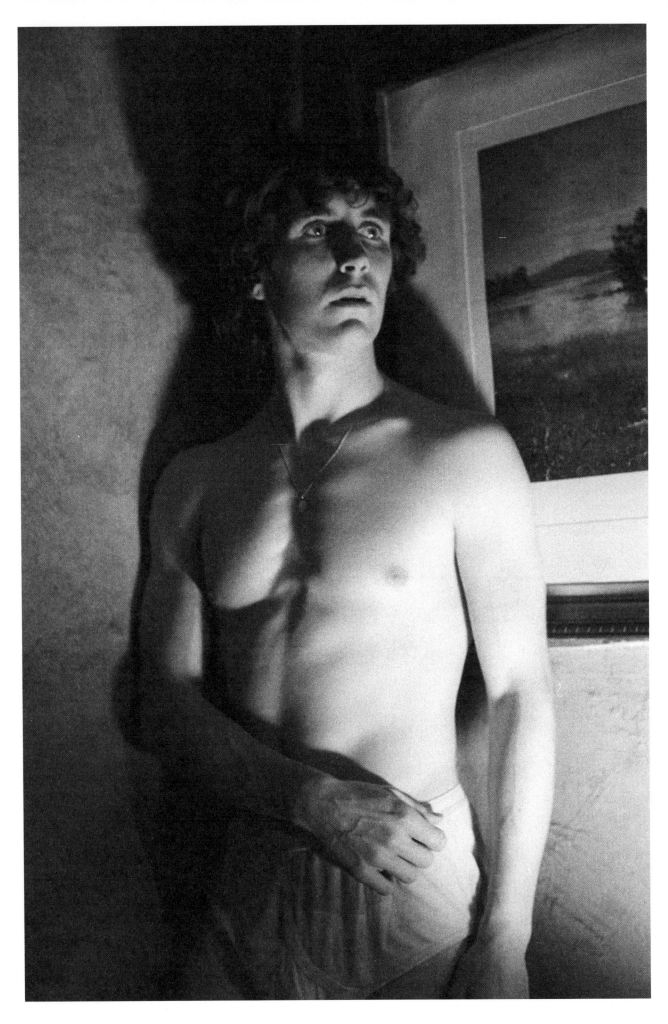

BRIEFS

When the first skimpy underwear for men was launched, it was a sensation. Unveiled in Chicago in 1935, the underpants were called Jockey briefs – the name hinting that they provided similar support to a jockstrap. Some 30,000 pairs were sold in the first three months – and within three years their manufacturer, Coopers Inc. (which would later change its name to Jockey) had seen this radical new design in men's underwear gain such wide acceptance that they could successfully launch them abroad. Early sales in the UK, where the briefs were known as Y-fronts, reached 30,000 pairs – a week.

It was a swimsuit from continental Europe that first inspired the idea for Jockey briefs. Coopers' vice president, Arthur Kneibler, received a postcard from the French Riviera and realized that the sleek, supportive swimsuit being worn by a man in the picture could be cut down to make a new kind of underwear – one that offered the support that, until then, no men's underwear did, apart from the so-called 'athletic supporters' worn by sportsmen. Add in Kneibler's idea for the Y-shaped front-fly opening, and the brief was born. It was such new territory that the patterns were developed in conjunction with urologists.

'I thought we had a winner here. Now I know we do,' noted Kneibler in a memo after the first sales figures were in. So great was demand that Coopers launched what it dubbed its 'Mascu-liner', an aircraft dedicated to making special deliveries of the briefs to stores all over the country.

The rise of the radical underwear was, however, not all plain sailing. What was radical for some was offensive for others, not least because the briefs revealed the full leg and, hugging the figure as they did, were less than discreet in their suggestion as to what they contained. In the late 1920s, modelling underwear had been considered downright scandalous, and in the mid-1930s, Jockey's models were still at pains to protect their identities, in some photographs even wearing face masks.

Opposite: British actor Paul McGann in a scene from *Withnail & I* (1987).
Above: An advertisement featuring a man who has it covered while playing football, thanks to his Wolsey X-fronts, from 1953.
Right: Men's underwear in its many forms and colours, 1970s-style, from a Jockey magazine advertisement.

Top: An advertisement on the Milan Metro featuring David Beckham modelling briefs for Armani.
Above: Construction moves on as a Calvin Klein model gazes on from a New York billboard, 1990s.

But Coopers was at pains to move society on. Prior to the launch of briefs, men's underwear was an under-the-counter purchase, such were the public's supposed sensitivities around suggestions of anything remotely related to genitalia. Jockeys became the first underwear to actually be displayed in store. It would be 1958, however, before the first Jockey commercial would air – on *The Tonight Show*, with host Jack Paar breaking down laughing as he attempted to expound the benefits of wearing briefs. The seemingly negative publicity, of course, ensured that Jockeys all but sold out nationwide the following day. By this time briefs were not only brief but colourful too, and even closer-fitting, in large part because of the development of new synthetic fabrics such as rayon, Dacron and DuPont's groundbreaking spandex. In 1959 Jockey launched the first low-rise bikini underwear for men too, made of 100 per cent stretch nylon.

Jockeys were also starting to divide the male populace between those who favoured briefs and those who considered themselves to be more of a boxers man. Certainly Jockey briefs won their ardent fans, artist Andy Warhol among them. He used one pair as a canvas for one of his dollar sign paintings, and would order his supply in bulk. And for him Jockey briefs, now with skimpier competitors, were brief enough: 'I told B I needed some socks too and at least 30 pairs of Jockey shorts,' he wrote in his *Philosophy of Andy Warhol (From A to B and Back Again)* (1975). 'He suggested I switch to Italian-style briefs, the ones with the T-shaped crotch that tends to build you up. I told him I'd tried them once, in Rome, the day I was walking through a Liz Taylor movie – and I didn't like them because they made me too self-aware. It gave me the feeling girls must have when they wear uplift bras.'

That feeling, however, would not stop other men from preferring ever more fitted styles. In the 1980s, with boxer shorts in the ascendant, Tom Cruise's appearance in a pair of 'tightie whities' (as briefs were nicknamed) in his breakthrough movie *Risky Business* (1983) led one fightback. By the 1990s, the athletic style of boxer–brief hybrid popularized by Calvin Klein had become a standard style of its own – ideal for those who, like Marky Mark (Mark Wahlberg) in its advertising, had a cast-iron six-pack stomach. Boxer briefs were also popular with those who liked to flash their brand loyalty: it became fashionable among youths for the briefs' logo-printed waistband to be worn visibly above the trousers. Who knows what the prudish underwear market might have made of that back in the 1930s?

I **Below:** Tight and blue – Jockey y-fronts of the 1960s.

Above: A golfer, in plus-fours and long argyle socks, scoops his ball out of a bunker.

SOCKS

The etiquette of men's dressing long had it that it was bad form for a man to show any part of his bare leg - so that when he sat down and crossed his legs, causing his trousers to rise, it was essential that his socks be long enough. Some men even resorted to wearing sock suspenders, which ensured that socks were pulled up tight at all times - contraptions largely made redundant by higher-quality, tighter elastic. The length of socks was in fact determined by the length of trousers: as trousers grew in length, replacing breeches or hose, so socks became shorter, replacing what had been in effect stockings. Those, indeed, were the dominant form of 'sock' from the Middle Ages onwards.

Men had long used some form of covering for the feet. In the eighth century BC, for example, the Greek poet Hesiod wrote in his *Works and Days* of foot coverings made from ox skin and felted animal hair, while the Romans wrapped their feet in strips of leather or fabric - although it was, at least initially, deemed rather unmanly for men in the military to do so. It is to the Romans of the second century AD that the first recognizable sock (the word comes from the Latin *soccus*) might be attributed. Theirs were made from a loose-fitting woven fabric and were pulled on and over rather than wrapped around the foot; worn under sandals, they became popular, not coincidentally perhaps, with the empire's expansion northwards into colder climes. Letters of the time speak of sending pairs of socks home to Rome.

But it was in the twelfth century that separate woven or sewn leg coverings became a matter of fashion. These were in coarsely sewn linens and wools for the less well-off, while the wealthy adopted velvets and colourful silks, often different for each leg, sometimes slashed to reveal another colour beneath, sometimes embroidered with emblems or even studded with jewels. Stretch was achieved by cutting the fabric on the bias, but the period also saw the advent of one of the first naturally elastic fine wool fabrics, called scarlet and typically dyed red - in fact, the fabric gave its name to the colour.

Below left: An advertisement for the Boston Garter sock, known all over the 'civilized' world, from 1903.
Below right: Preppy fashion of 1953 dicatated that the wearing of knee-length socks with your shorts was the done thing.

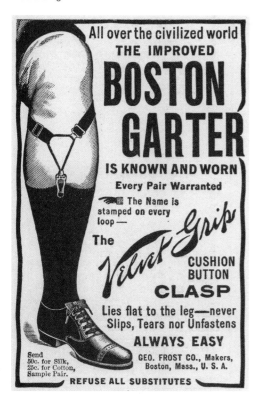

I Above: Jack Lemmon relaxing in 1956.

These stockings were worn with short breeches, an evolution of the cross-gartered full-length leather leg coverings worn previously, and were thus more a viable focus for matters of style, and most especially of style for men, since women wore floor-length dresses. The physical appeal of a man, indeed, might be determined less by the size of his biceps as by the shapeliness of his legs.

In 1589 – by which point two stockings had become one garment – Englishman William Lee invented the first dedicated wool hosiery knitting machine. Queen Elizabeth I is said to have refused to grant him what then amounted to a patent on his device because, used to wearing expensive imported silks, she found woollen stockings too coarse.

Such machines, however, were commonplace by the end of the century and allowed wool stockings of all kinds to become an element of dress for everyone, with greater comfort achieved with the advent of the first cotton stockings in the late seventeenth century. Such manufacturing also allowed for a faster change of pace in fashions. As men's breeches headed towards knee-length, for example, stockings shortened accordingly and began to resemble more refined versions of the socks the Romans had worn more than a millennium previously.

Despite socks getting ever shorter as leg coverings grew longer, dress etiquette's focus on them has remained: socks should match either one's trousers or one's shoes, but never neither. And so has their place as a site of personal expression and fashion: although by the early twentieth century men's socks were available in any combination of colours and patterns, some have won particular attention.

So-called argyle socks, for example, originated in Highland dress, being knitted in the same tartan patterns as kilts (although it was considered stylish not to match the two), with the Clan Campbell – of which the Duke of Argyll is chief – favouring a diamond pattern. Scottish knitwear manufacturer Pringle used the Campbell tartan in sweaters and socks in the 1920s and, thanks to the Duke of Windsor buying them to play golf in, they soon became widely fashionable. The diamond sock pattern went international when the president of the American men's outfitters Brooks Brothers visited the UK in 1949, saw golfers so attired, and decided to stock the patterned sock in his stores back home.

Below: Will.i.am of the Black Eyed Peas arrives at the 2005 MTV Video Music Awards in Miami.

THE VEST

If popular culture can make a fashion, so too can it break one. Until *It Happened One Night*, a movie with Clark Gable released in 1934, it had been commonplace for a man to wear a vest, or singlet or tank top (named differently in different parts of the world), as part of his underwear. This was a time before air conditioning and central heating, so the vest functioned as either an absorbent or an insulating layer, depending on the climate. But then Gable removed his shirt and revealed a bare chest – and suddenly men began to question just why they wore a vest at all. Doing so became a choice rather than an expectation. Certainly sales plummeted, recovering only with the advent of World War II, when the T-shirt style of undershirt was part of standard-issue uniform for American and British troops alike.

Yet what sex appeal the vest had did not fade altogether, especially when it was later sometimes called a 'muscle shirt' for the way it emphasized the male physique, making it popular with body-builders ever since competitions were first held. Indeed, cinema itself countered with *A Streetcar Named Desire* in 1951, with Marlon Brando playing über-male Stanley Kowalski in a white vest that would literally be torn from him in a moment of high erotic charge. The vest became a visual shorthand in many, often period, films, for a working man in private, either shirtless and exposed with his guard down, or shirtless and ready for action. *Bonnie & Clyde* (1967), *The Sting* (1973), *Raging Bull* (1980) and the *Rambo* (from 1982) and *Die Hard* series (from 1988) showcase the vest in this sense.

The white vest in particular became notably indicative of an Italian-American working-class masculinity. This was sometimes portrayed as being unrefined and brutish – and not for nothing has this piece of underwear also, since the 1970s, been unappealingly dubbed the 'wife-beater' shirt, an association with domestic violence often reinforced by the characters who have worn it in various movies.

In the 1990s the white vest became part of Cholo street style, a look adopted specifically by gang members of Mexican descent (though the term was also applied to Hispanics and Filipinos) in the American Southwest – from California to Colorado and south to New Mexico – blending skater and hip hop references. The garment would typically be worn under outsize short-sleeved work or plaid flannel shirts, typically done up only at the neck so that the vest was in part on show.

The vest or tank top's origins, however, go back to the 1880s, when it was worn for athletics, in particular gymnastics, its sleeveless nature giving the wearer a full range of motion in the arms. (The tank top takes its name from the tank suit style of swimwear popular in the 1920s, itself so named for its use in a swimming tank or pool.)

In 1933 another variant on the style, the string vest, was invented by Henrik Brun, a commandant in the Norwegian army, who fashioned his prototype for the garment from two fine fishing nets. Brun had correctly surmised that the open weave would trap warm air close to the body. Thanks to the adoption of the string vest by King Haakon VII of Norway, the style soon became a national fashion.

During the 1950s, the British War Office conducted a series of tests to find out whether the string vest could prove a suitable garment for its troops. Soldiers of the Royal Warwickshire Regiment were ordered to wear three different types of undershirt beneath their jackets throughout the two hottest summer months in the Canal Zone of Egypt – and concluded that the string vest kept them coolest. Yet apparently only two of the soldiers chose to continue to wear a string vest after the conclusion of the tests. 'Seemingly all vests were to be regarded with suspicion,' the report noted. At least the string vest would have some future as an outerwear garment, popular with Rastafarians and punks.

Below: Marlon Brando, giving the 'wife beater' sex appeal in a publicity shot for the movie of *A Streetcar Named Desire* (1951).
Opposite: Bruce Willis as Detective John McLane in *Die Hard: With a Vengeance* (1995).

PYJAMAS

The loose, light and comfortable nature of pyjamas might well suggest their origins in a warm climate, and indeed, proto-pyjamas (from *pāy* and *jāma*, Persian words meaning 'leg' and 'clothing') were worn throughout India and Asia for at least two centuries before colonialists from the West discovered them. Appreciating the practicality of these drawstring trousers combined with the traditional nightshirt – here was a garment that, under a dressing gown, could be worn respectably around the home – from the 1870s men in Great Britain, especially, began wearing them.

Such was the Victorian fashion for pyjamas that within 20 years, by which point the familiar two-piece set of trousers and tunic was established, winter-weight styles in silk or wool were also being worn and the nightshirt was on its way out. By the 1930s pyjamas had become the staple attire for bed, with men choosing styles in cool cottons, calico or cosy flannelette, depending on the season. By then, thanks in large part to Coco Chanel's enthusiasm for reinventing menswear for women to wear, pyjamas had come to be regarded as unisex.

Pyjamas in pale-blue stripes were quickly deemed to be the most classic of styles. Bolder styles included those in a paisley print, which, although originating with the Sassanid dynasty in Iran, was widely considered to be a nod to the pyjama's Indian origins. Certainly pyjamas' more outlandish styles were embraced by many men, a more privately expressive alternative to masculine daywear, which remained largely dark and conservative. Warren Harding, American president during the 1920s, favoured a pair in turquoise silk with appliquéd white leaves.

But the real boost to their popularity came from their public image. From the pre-World War II years through the 1950s pyjamas would be worn by a host of Hollywood stars. Noël Coward was happy to be caught wearing them in candid portraits, complete with monogrammed dressing gown and cigarette in a holder, making the wearing of pyjamas outside the bedroom and into

Opposite: *Playboy* founder Hugh Hefner relaxes at home – with pet bunny – in Brentwood, California, 2001.
Below: Paul Newman, in PJs, as the washed-up football star in the movie of *Cat on a Hot Tin Roof* (1958), with Elizabeth Taylor.

daylight hours the epitome of style for the gentleman of leisure. *Playboy* founder Hugh Hefner was another who realized this, making the look his signature. Style benchmark Cary Grant wore pyjamas for scenes in several movies, including *Indiscreet* (1958); Marlon Brando wore them in *A Streetcar Named Desire* (1951); and incapacity proved the perfect opportunity to lounge around in them, as Jimmy Stewart did in *Rear Window* (1954) and Paul Newman did in *Cat on a Hot Tin Roof* (1958).

Less glamorously, in 1951 *The Charleville Times*, an Australian newspaper, reported on what came to be dubbed the Pyjama War – a spate of fist-fights breaking out between residents of the male ward of the St Camillus hospital in Limerick, Ireland. The paper reported that 'an old inmate, neatly clad in pyjamas and slippers, jeered at the shiny shanks of another inmate, who shuffled by in a flowing, sloppy nightshirt', while those in nightshirts 'scoffed at the old men with pot bellies in fancy sleeping pants.' When the threat to withdraw the men's tobacco allowance failed to prevent further scuffles, 'Limerick City Council stepped in and decided to hold an inquiry into the long-standing problem: are pyjamas better than nightshirts?' Unfortunately the record does not show what conclusion it reached.

The appeal of pyjamas was not lost on later generations. The artist Julian Schnabel took to wearing (often paint-splattered) silk pyjamas day and night, despite what he saw as the less positive ways in which this might be viewed. 'When you see somebody walking down the street in pyjamas, they think you just got out of a mental hospital,' he said in an interview in 2008. 'When my boys were born, I was in the maternity ward and I was walking around in my pajamas. And a lady said to me, "You're on the wrong floor." I said, "No, no, no, I'm not. I have these kids." She said, "You can't walk around in your pajamas." And some woman who was a painter said, "That's Julian Schnabel. He walks around in his pyjamas. It's okay."' In 2012 Caddo Parish in Louisiana, USA, even proposed an ordnance prohibiting people from wearing pyjamas in public, seeing this as an affront to the community's 'moral fibre'.

If the 1950s were a high point for pyjamas' popularity, over the following decades they would move in and out of fashion. Pyjamas would by turns be considered dapper, crisp and clean, or fuddy-duddy.

Opposite: Jimmy Stewart as the invalid with an uneasy hunch in Alfred Hitchcock's *Rear Window* (1954)
Below: Rod Stewart, resting from rocking, in 1974.

SWIMWEAR

Men's swimwear has evolved since the late nineteenth century with three main concerns: style, fabric innovation and a varying societal fear of any degree of public nudity. And arguably the latter has been the most influential.

The 1970s might have glimpsed what there was of designer Rudi Gernreich's first thong for a man, but the adoption of small, figure-hugging nylon briefs by the more daring man in the professional swimming arena had begun in 1960, when designer Peter Travis created the style for Australian company Speedo. The trick, he said, was to position the briefs on the hips, not at the waist, and cut the sides high, all the better for swimming in. All the same, the first man to wear them on Sydney's Bondi Beach was arrested (but not charged, because no pubic hair was on show).

But if the modern era has settled largely on the comfort, practicality and discretion of board shorts as offering the best of all worlds, a century beforehand a man would have been encumbered by what was effectively a knitted woollen body-suit. This protected his modesty – and the blushes of delicate lady onlookers – but weighed several kilos when wet and made actual swimming a potentially dangerous business.

Indeed, prior to the 1860s a man would swim, if he swam at all, naked – a libertine habit that society could not, of course, allow for long. In 1869 Frédéric Bazille's painting *Scène d'été* depicted a kind of surprisingly modern swimwear that was both newfangled and strictly for wearing in private and only in the company of men. Public bathing, especially if women were present, required much more covering up, although diehard male recreational swimmers often defied the regulation: men swam naked each morning in London's Hyde Park until as late as 1906.

In the 1920s – an era of innovation in technology, art and revolutionary thinking – most swimwear was, in the United States, defined by the American Association of Park Superintendents' 'Bathing Suit Regulations', published in *The American City* in 1917, and these determined that even men's bathing suits, now cut to the top of the leg, required some kind of skirting effect to cover the trunks. The legs of the trunks, meanwhile, could end no more than 10 centimetres (4 inches) from the knee. And the guardians of decency thought of everything: flesh-coloured swimsuits were also prohibited.

It was innovation more in cut and cloth than in styling – the deep armholes and closed-leg trunks of the one-piece 'speed suit' for example, or the introduction of Lastex, a new synthetic-rubber yarn – that did most to move men's swimwear on and to look more athletic. Yet for all that, swimwear would remain one-piece until at least the pre-World War II years. Although attempts were made, from 1933, to introduce the 'men's topper' (a swimsuit with a streamlined, vest-like top half that could be unzipped from the trunks), for a man to bare his chest was to risk accusation of indecent exposure. It was not until 1937 that swimwear finally exposed the chest and focused on the provision of simple, streamlined trunks.

Opposite: Swimming champions Johnny Weissmuller (who would later play Tarzan) and Duke Kahanamoku – pioneer of swim shorts – pose in their swimsuits around 1924.
Below: Welsh singer Tom Jones, sans medallion but in macho man pose, in 1968.

The idea came from France and a company called BVD. And its good fortune had been to hire the Olympic swimmer and 'Aquadonis' Johnny Weissmuller as a model and adviser in 1929 – the man who in 1932 would win a seven-year contract with Metro-Goldwyn-Mayer to play Tarzan, a role that would make him (and his choice of swimwear) internationally famous. The idea spread slowly, however; by the late 1940s half-hearted off-the-shoulder-style one-piece swimsuits for men were not uncommon. But when the chest was finally fully bared, the suntan so fashionable since the 1930s could finally be achieved.

Ironically perhaps, the style of trunks that first appeared was form-fitting – with supports sewn right in, meaning that men no longer had to wear underwear under their swimwear. This was deemed to give them a smart, smooth appearance but perhaps also left little to the imagination, not to mention sometimes offering a challenge to straight faces, as seen in swimwear manufacturer Jantzen's 1947 campaign starring young actor James Garner: its high-waisted 'savage swim trunks' came in a waffle weave, with a flap pocket to the front, and resembled an outsize nappy. Other attempts to give swim trunks a sartorial edge included a fly-front and even a contrast-coloured buckled belt – neither idea stuck.

It took the cool of surfing, and its practical need for a greater ease of movement, to introduce a looser style. The shift to what might pass as the first modern form of swimwear came in the 1950s, when high-waisted, lace-up board shorts were popularized by Hawaiian surf pioneer and Olympic swimmer Duke Kahanamoku. Minoru Nii, a tailor based near the Hawaiian surfing mecca of Makaha, made the 'Makaha Drowners' that would transcend the surfing community.

Celebrities such as surfer Richard Boone and Rat Pack actor Peter Lawford soon took to board shorts, although the publicity surrounding their being worn by John F. Kennedy no doubt had more effect on the burgeoning middle classes looking to holiday on the beach or away in exotic locations. Worn with a matching towelling-lined cabana shirt, board shorts were sufficiently smart and discreet to wear for pool-side cocktails. They could even be bought in denim or needle corduroy.

But swimwear had not stopped its advance at drinks with umbrellas. Swimwear company Jantzen was quick to become the first to sponsor a surfer, Ricky Grigg, while competing makers would seek to nose ahead through technical innovation. Now that there was a more sport-oriented use for swim shorts, rather than their being worn for leisure swimming, advances in performance became increasingly important: Hang Ten devised the first fast-drying nylon shorts, for example. Many further wonder fabrics would follow them into the water.

Below: Champion swimmer Michael Phelps, at the 2012 London Olympic Games.

Above: Elvis Presley poses uneasily on a surfboard for a publicity shot for *Blue Hawaii* (1961).

6.
WATCHES &
JEWELLERY

CUFFLINKS / THE DIVING WATCH / THE PILOT'S WATCH / THE SIGNET RING

CUFFLINKS

Men have used some form of linking device, of various degrees of craft and sophistication, to tighten the ends of their sleeves since at least ancient Egyptian times – even if the more extravagant examples were often more symbolic than practical. 'Sleeve buttons' or ribbons were, from medieval times, worn to commemorate a royal event and were often given as gifts, a tradition that survives in the idea that no man should buy his own cufflinks, but rather they should be a present to mark a special occasion. Shirts requiring the fastening of a distinct cuff can be dated to the late seventeenth and early eighteenth century and with them came the rise of more considered means of fastening.

Despite limitations on their design – they cannot be too big, they must fit through a buttonhole, and so on – styles of cufflink have, over the centuries, varied enormously. They have ranged from simple ribbons to silk knots; from two-piece models that snap together to those with a decorative outer and a swivelling T-bar section that allows it to be pushed through and fastened behind the buttonhole; from the ornate to the novelty; from those made from plain and base materials to those that are extravagant and jewel-encrusted.

Despite their royal associations, not every royal chose to wear them. France's Louis XIV (1638–1715), for example, had an extravagant love of diamonds, owning some 104 diamond buttons and 48 diamond studs, but in his sleeves he wore ribbons. Towards the end of his reign, some members of his court – the setters of fashion – began to wear chain-linked pairs of identical buttons, often set with painted miniatures, to fasten their sleeves. The earliest sighting of a pair of diamond cuff buttons recorded in print appeared in an issue of the *London Gazette* in 1684.

Above: Yellow silk knots from shirtmakers Hilditch & Key on London's Jermyn Street.
Right: The presidential cobalt-bue cufflinks – featuring a gold-plated presidential eagle and, on the reverse, the signature of the incumbent president – are among the most sought-after of accessories.

Some have attributed the moment at which cufflinks became a genuine subject of fashion to the runaway success of Alexandre Dumas's *The Count of Monte Cristo* (1844), in which the Baron Danglars, one of the main protagonists, is described as wearing his cuffs turned back in order to show off what kept them pinned in place: 'an enormous diamond that glittered in his shirt, and the red ribbon that depended from his button hole.' Apocryphal though it may be, the story has it that French tailors were so enamoured of this character's style that they encouraged the adoption of what would come to be known as the French, or double, cuff in order that their gentlemen clients would have another opportunity to express their wealth and sophistication. The wearing of cufflinks spread from aristocrats to the everyman looking to distinguish himself – and with the timely ability of industry to mass-produce such items, and to electroplate base metals, the market was ready to provide.

Cufflinks brought with them a shift in dress etiquette too. For much of its history the shirt was worn as an undergarment and revealing any part of it considered a faux pas; now tailors began to cut the sleeve of a jacket sufficiently short to reveal just a few centimetres of shirt cuff, and with it,

the cufflinks. Laundering methods also encouraged the wearing of cufflinks: in the Victorian period, shirt collars and cuffs were starched very stiff, which made a standard button fastening difficult and necessitated the use of links. Links became indicative of the wearer's formal propriety, so much so that few shirts with a button cuff fastening were available to purchase even should a man want one.

But the writing was on the wall. It was said to be the Duke of Windsor, a figure of great influence in men's attire, who with his embracing of a more American, casual way of dressing during the 1930s brought in the decline of cufflinks as a necessity of the male wardrobe. This left them to be worn only in the still-regimented setting of work, or on formal occasions that required black-tie dinner dress.

Yet cufflinks would not die out altogether: they witnessed a revival during the 1950s with the 'stirrup' style, for example, a curved bar that wrapped around the outer edge of the shirt cuff; and in the 1960s, when the wearing of double-sided links became the done thing.

The 1930s had seen other signs of the decline of the cufflink as a serious sartorial item too, with the advent of the first novelty pair, attributed to jewellery designer Paul Flato. Having forgotten his cufflinks, Flato made use of two small brass bolts and screws instead; the popular US pianist Eddie Duchin was so impressed that he commissioned a pair in gold. A world of enamel road signs, gothic death's heads and other supposedly witty alternatives would later follow.

Opposite: The British comic actor Dudley Moore, at home in London in 1967

THE DIVING WATCH

When 100 metres (330 feet) below the surface is considered the outer limit for recreational scuba diving – and the safe diving limit for amateurs is a mere 40 metres (130 feet) – it is easy to see that diving watches capable of operating at thousands of metres under the water evoke a certain appreciation of their technical marvel, all the more pronounced if the watch is a mechanical one.

Indeed, watchmakers appear to be on a continual quest to outdo each other. When IWC launched its Ocean 2000 in 1980 (the result of a design collaboration with Porsche), it set a new, awe-inspiring benchmark in water resistance, to 200 atmospheres or 2,000 metres (6,560 feet) below. Breitling then produced its Avenger Seawolf, water-resistant to a staggering 3,000 metres (9,840 feet). Finally, by filling the case of its Hydro Challenger with a special transparent oil-like substance that allowed the dial to be read at any angle, in 1997 Bell & Ross created a record-breaking watch that could withstand the pressures of operating at the bottom of the Mariana Trench – the deepest point on Earth at around 11,000 metres (36,090 feet) under the sea.

Such a professional performance capability is unlikely to be employed by the vast majority of these watches' wearers – but the mere suggestion that they have such impressive robustness provides a frisson of manly excitement. The necessity to withstand such pressure is why most diving watches are made of steel (though in a satin finish for professional use, shiny parts being known to attract barracudas), titanium (following the Ocean 2000), or the latest polymers. Rubber or synthetic seals are required at any point where the case may be opened, such as at the case back, crown and sometimes between crystal and case. And on deeper-water models a helium escape valve is required to let out compressed gases and prevent the watch from literally exploding after a rapid ascent. Indeed, in order to be certified 'professional' a diving watch must have this, or a similar device, together with a unidirectional bezel, luminous markings on dial and bezel, a screw-in crown and time display with second hand, and be water-resistant to 300 metres (985 feet) or more.

Opposite: The Rolex Deepsea, among the most distinctive of all diving watches.
Below: A US Navy diver carries the essentials on his wrists – a diving watch, depth card and compass.

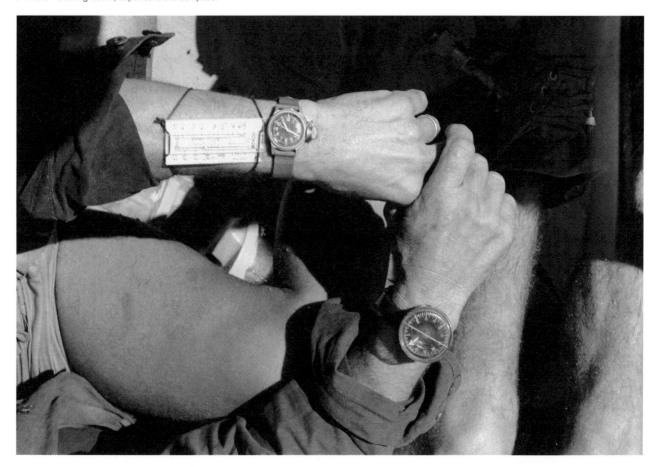

The diving watch has taken many decades of development to reach current levels of advancement. Early developments in waterproofing began in the 1920s, essentially as a means of ensuring reliability. Rolex patented the first Oyster dust- and water-resistant wristwatch in 1926. Assisted by some heavy marketing – Mercedes Gleitze swimming across the English Channel with her Rolex; window displays showing a watch ticking inside a tank of water – the idea of a water-resistant wristwatch had finally taken hold by the 1930s, when Omega (maker of the famous Seamaster) launched its Marine.

But, as with so many technical advances, it was war, or the threat of it, that provided the impetus to design a watch capable of operating at depth. Panerai, originally a manufacturer of general military hardware, created an outsized diving watch for Italian commandos, with many other companies developing diving watches for various nations' armed forces during World War II and its aftermath. Blancpain, for instance, found itself charged by French naval officers Robert Maloubier and Claude Riffaud, creators of the elite Nageurs de Combat (combat swimmers) unit, to make a watch that would meet their demanding specifications. The result, in 1953, was the Fifty Fathoms, which was also adopted by forces in the United States, Germany and Israel. More recently, IWC's first use of titanium was the result of a request from the German Navy in the 1980s to develop an anti-magnetic watch for its mine-sweeping divers. Diving watches remain part of standard-issue kit for submariners and naval officers.

The development of the Aqua-Lung by legendary diver Jacques Cousteau and engineer Émile Gagnan in 1942 had led to the birth of scuba-diving as a leisure activity rather than a purely professional one and created a whole new market for diving watches. In 1953, after extensive trials with professional divers, Rolex launched its Submariner, the first watch (only just) with a rotating bezel – and arguably the classic of the form. By the 1960s the company was also testing its Sea-Dweller 2000 with the divers of COMEX, the French specialists in commercial diving, notably for the oil industry. Exploration for oil during this period, especially in the North Sea, was also a factor in boosting demand for diving watches; other, of course, than the inconvenience of having to take a normal watch off at the beach.

Opposite: Omega's Ploprof takes it name from the first letters of *plongeur* (diver) and *professionel* and was launched in 1970.
Below: A modern iteration of Omega's iconic Seamaster model.

THE PILOT'S WATCH

In an age of computerization, it is perhaps a surprise that a watch is still thought to be a practical necessity for a pilot. Certainly, although there have been exceptions during wartime, historically watches have rarely been a standard-issue item for military or commercial pilots. As late as the Vietnam era, combat pilots often wore their own watch and carried a stopwatch for navigational duties.

And yet any number of the major watch manufacturers of the twentieth century have offered their version of a watch designed with pilots in mind: Longines' Swissair model of 1943; Benrus's wonderfully named Sky Chief of the same era; Glycine's Airman automatic; the Zenith Pilot of the mid-1950s; Rolex's Air King and Omega's Speedmaster; as well as those from companies that have won a reputation for specializing in the field, among them Fortis, IWC – with its iconic Mark XI watch of 1948 and subsequent variations – and Breitling, with its Aerospace and Navitimer models, the latter being the oldest chronograph in continuous production since its launch around 1952.

Accurate timekeeping is essential for celestial navigation, especially over sea or when landmarks are no longer visible. Indeed, the very first wristwatch was made for a flyer. Cartier worked to a commission from the dashing Brazilian aviator Alberto Santos-Dumont for a watch he would be able to see easily without having to pull it from his pocket under heavy-duty leather layers. It was subsequently known and sold as the Santos.

The pilot's watch has a certain timeless, romantic machismo that, bolstered by the perceived glamour of daring wartime exploits, has seen it widely worn by men who come closest to a cockpit only when they take a wrong turn into first class. Its defining characteristics are simplicity of design, a larger dial with absolute legibility in its arrangement (early versions were viewed through goggles), luminous hands, typically a white-on-black colourway, and an ability to perform in tough conditions. Some 60 or more years ago, that meant having to contend with exposure to strong vibrations and outside temperatures of -44°C (-47°F), as pilot Roland Rohlfs discovered when he flew at a record height of 10,500 metres (34,500 feet) in 1919 and lived to tell both the tale and the time. As well as being robust, early pilot's watches had the perhaps unexpected benefit of being waterproof, to protect the innards as much from grime as from the moisture that forms over surfaces in an unpressurized environment at altitude. Later, the watch was made with glass that could survive sudden depressurization.

In 1931 Charles Lindbergh – having had the unfortunate experience of finding that his watch had expired halfway through his record-breaking transatlantic flight persuaded Longines to create a watch to his specifications: the Hour Angle watch had a non-slip outsize bezel with a zero mark, allowing easier timing of compass transmitter wayfinding signals, and a crown that enabled it to be operated with gloves.

I Left: IWC Mark II, from 1948.

The military look of the dial remained. By World War II one of the most popular standard-issue airmen's watches was the A-11. This long-serving timepiece had large white luminous Arabic numerals and hands on a matt black background. It was a look that echoed that of aircraft dashboards. Indeed, the A-11's was a functional, almost minimalist style that was coming to define what a pilot's watch should look like. The look had also been adopted by IWC when it launched its first dedicated pilot's watch in 1936, which also came with an inlaid arrow for short interval timing. This watch took its inspiration from a German aircraft, the Junkers JU 52, whose interior and cockpit was partly styled along lines suggested by the legendary Bauhaus designer Marcel Breuer.

The IWC Mark XI was perhaps the first watch to consider from the inside out the issues involved in flying: although Vacheron Constantin and Tissot had both developed anti-magnetic watches much earlier, in 1915 and 1929 respectively, it was IWC that realized the importance of this to flyers. The Mark XI had an additional inner, highly conductive case made of soft iron ore to screen the movement from the strong magnetic fields experienced in the cockpit, which could make a timepiece run fast or slow – or even make it stop altogether.

Other functions specifically aimed at aviators would be added to the evolving idea of what constituted a pilot's watch. The most useful development was the chronograph. Gaston Breitling, founder of Breitling, had created the first wristwatch chronograph in 1915, with the first independent chronograph pushpiece to control start/stop and return-to-zero following in 1923, and the second return-to-zero pushpiece following in 1934. This was an addition of genuine use to pilots, used to measure elapsed flight time and hence remaining fuel, as well as for more accurate measurement of compass transmissions for navigation. That said, in regions where no compass transmissions could be received and celestial navigation was essential, the favoured timepieces deliberately had no chronograph function because its use impaired the watch's timekeeping. Knowing where you were going somehow seemed more important than knowing if you could make it there.

Left: Breitling's Navitimer, the first pilot's watch to incorporate an indispensable slide-rule function.

THE SIGNET RING

Above: A close-up of the clasped hands – and signet ring – of the Prince of Wales, on a visit to New Zealand in 2005.
Below: Robert Montgomery in a publicity still for *Ride the Pink Horse* (1947).

Examine the hands of the men of ruling castes, from European aristocracy through to political players and members of American WASPish clans, and there one might find a distinctive oval- or square-faced ring. The Pope wears one, called the Ring of the Fisherman, which is duly kissed on meeting him as a sign of allegiance or submission. Depending on the country, it might be found on the little finger of one hand or the other, as etiquette dictates to be proper in Britain and the United States, for example (although Winston Churchill bucked this by wearing his on his wedding-ring finger). But whatever finger it is on, this seemingly insignificant adornment says clearly that its wearer is someone.

The gold, silver or carved stone signet ring was a functional as much as a decorative item as long ago as the time of the ancient Egyptians, but became more widely worn in Europe in the Middle Ages, a period when men readily wore jewellery but when few men could write. The engraved surface – known as intaglio – of the ring bore the family crest or coat of arms and, in lieu of a written signature, it was plunged into a small pool of warm sealing wax placed on a document to act as authentification or fastening. The fact that these rings had to stand up to this frequent use, and were often passed down through the generations, meant they tended to be considerable pieces of jewellery. By the early nineteenth century, not only could more men write, but such personal seals were worn as ornamental mounts strung as a fob from a pocket chain, thus signalling the fall of the signet ring from favour.

At least, for a while. If the signet ring lost its physical heft and function, it retained a symbolic one. Possessing a family crest or coat of arms indicated that one was a man of rank, of good family, of power – and the ring proved the ideal way to display this fact. Gentlemen donned the family heirloom, as Franklin D. Roosevelt wore his father's, and which he in turn would hand on to his eldest son, James. If newly titled, men had a signet ring made in order to display their coat of arms, or if not quite of sufficiently high rank to have one of those, to show off their initials in some decorative scrollwork.

Some men even designed their own symbols, a kind of personal brand, usually inspired by motifs from the Renaissance, sometimes taking symbols reflecting their military service or an interest in the arts or sciences. The very wealthy had their emblem carved into a precious and usually dark stone, such as amethyst, ruby or lapis lazuli. Since the signet ring was no longer typically required to make an impression in wax, some gentlemen had their rings made with a relief carving, or cameo.

Whatever form it took, the signet ring was imbued with special significance. While the decorum of men's dress of the time was such that they were free to wear multiple rings, and other jewellery, if they chose, only the signet ring was considered to be an essential finishing touch for a gentleman to be considered properly dressed. Even when the wearing of jewellery by men began to fall out of fashion, around the 1850s, still the signet ring remained an essential, so much so that even men whom society deemed not entitled to wear a signet ring – that is, non-gentlemen, however wealthy they might be – began to wear one too. This had the effect of somewhat denting the ring's cachet.

Indeed, by the twentieth century, the signet ring had attained a dual identity. It remained a marker of men of rank, yet it also became a marker of men of no rank at all, or at least only of a rank that was self-made. In keeping with the century's sartorial imitation of the well-to-do by the hoi polloi, the signet ring – along with the slimmer-line pinkie ring and its hefty, almost parodic cousin, the sovereign ring – came to be worn by the less than aristocratic, from mafiosi such as 1930s gangster Charles 'Lucky' Luciano to stars of show business's golden era such as Bob Hope, Jack Benny and Frank Sinatra (who once refused the gift of an ID bracelet from his family, saying he only wore his family-crested ring) to rappers and even the archetypal second-hand car salesman. It even, perhaps, came to suggest a touch of vulgarity.

Above: Former baseball player and later manager of the New York Yankees, Joe Torre, with a sizable and ornate signet ring, in 1996.

7.
BAGS

THE BRIEFCASE / THE RUCKSACK / THE SATCHEL

THE BRIEFCASE

The attaché case or briefcase has always implied more than its lack of a capacious interior suggests. It is the bag of the salaryman, crawling his way up the greasy pole in his identikit business uniform; it is the bag of the lawyer, arriving to discuss terms; it is the bag of the academic, stuffed full of crumpled papers; it is the bag with the bomb, discreetly left abandoned under the table – as Colonel Claus von Stauffenberg left his in Hitler's planning room at the Wolf's Lair in Prussia in 1944 in the July bomb plot. And it is the bag in which the British annual budget documents are famously carried by the Chancellor of the Exchequer, in a ritual that underlines the style's inherent formality.

It was in 1860 that the red briefcase was first used to carry the paperwork that would enable the Chancellor to present the government's intentions regarding matters of taxation and spending. It became a tradition that has been upheld every year since, with an exception in the early 1990s, when Chancellor Norman Lamont used the budget briefcase to carry, hidden away, a bottle of Highland Park whisky while his parliamentary private secretary carried the budget papers in a folder under his arm.

Above: A tan briefcase from the British leather-goods designer Bill Amberg.
Below: Neville Chamberlain, Britain's Chancellor of the Exchequer in 1923, holding the red budget case.
Opposite: A familiar sight in 'The City', as London's financial district is known, until the late 1970s – a bowler-hatted, briefcase-carrying 'city gent', pictured here in 1972.

The original briefcase that was used to carry the budget papers was made of red leather on pine, lined with black satin and complete with the letters VR, for Victoria Regina, on its side. It was used until 2010, when it was retired, having become too frail for further use. It had been made by London company Barrow and Gale for the nineteenth-century chancellor William Gladstone, for whom it was said at the time, by the journal *London Society*, to be just one of 'a series of stage accessories' with which he made his notoriously long speeches. The briefcase has the same potential for show and symbolism even today: seeing it lifted on to a table and its fastenings opened with loud clicks surely inspires in its onlookers a sense of anticipation, if not foreboding, that the same action performed with any other bag cannot achieve. The journal wrote of 'that ominous box – that box which by many was expected to prove the horn of plenty, and by others a very Pandora's box, without even hope at the bottom.'

The red briefcase, indeed, was just one of a family of red briefcases made by the company for British ministers since the early nineteenth century. It was also a tradition that spread: a red briefcase has on occasion been part of the ceremony of Budget Day in India, for example, in a throwback to colonial days. Certainly, the briefcase has historic connections to the world of money, descending as it does from a satchel-type bag used in the fourteenth century to carry money and known as a *bougette* (French for 'small bag', and also the origin of the word 'budget').

The bag style's later use had more legalistic overtones: the first form of the briefcase was used in the eighteenth century when people attempted to carry important legal documents flat between thin metal sheets. Finding this both cumbersome and uncomfortable, clerks and solicitors began to commission saddlemakers to produce a case in which the documents – or briefs, in legalese – could be carried. In the early twentieth century, not only was the briefcase widely used in office business of all sorts, but the French and Italian leather-goods industries then in the ascendant began to produce their own, more upmarket versions. These were typically bigger and had multiple inner sections, so that alongside one's paperwork one could also carry, perhaps, lunch or a fresh shirt.

By the 1950s and 1960s, the smartness of one's briefcase became a measure of one's ambition in the world of work as much as one's suit or shoes. But that also marked the briefcase's slow decline in the face of demand for more broadly utilitarian means of carriage. In the modern era, the briefcase might have seemed destined for another revival, being almost the perfect shape and offering the right solidity in which to safely carry a laptop or tablet. But changing lifestyles have meant that – the occasional moment in fashion aside – it was not to be. Case closed.

THE RUCKSACK

The rucksack conjours up images of *Boy's Own* travels, of self-sufficient backwoodsmen tramping through unknown territories, of the freedom of the open road – the forward momentum of adventure such that one definitely needs one's hands free to explore. It has become the bag of choice not only of pioneers but also of trekkers and soldiers. Indeed, trials for elite regiments often involve the challenge of marching long distances in harsh conditions carrying heavy packs. In the UK, members of the Parachute Regiment were celebrated for doing just this across the Falkland Islands in their defence against Argentinian invasion in 1982 – 'yomping' was the term given to such a fully loaded march.

People have, of course, carried their belongings on their backs since first having anything to carry. The rucksack (from the German *Rücken*, meaning 'back') or backpack (a term coined in the United States during the 1910s) is at least 5,000 years old: a body dating to around 3300 BC that had been preserved in the ice of the Alps was discovered together with what looked remarkably like a modern backpack. Native American tribes are also known to have used a similar style.

But its use in modern times dates to late nineteenth-century Norway, where skiing long distances between remote villages necessitated the practicality of the rucksack's style. It was there known as a *sekk med meis*, or 'bag with a frame' – for it is a bag mounted on a loadbearing frame, thereby increasing the amount of belongings that can be carried. In 1886, the first patent for a metal-framed backpack was filed by a Colonel Merriam, with Norwegian Ole Bergan filing the next patent on a design in 1909.

In 1922, Lloyd F. Nelson patented his wooden-frame-based Trapper style, a design he was inspired to create after hiking across Alaska using an uncomfortable Inuit-made 'sticks-and-sealskin' backpack two years earlier. He proved the efficacy of his own design by posing wearing the Trapper with his young daughter Lois in it. Unfortunately for Nelson, the timing was off: although he launched his rucksack commercially in the mid-1920s, he sold the business just before hiking took off as a popular weekend and holiday activity. Not long after the sale, the Boy Scouts of America embraced the design and helped spark a national fondness for the outdoor life.

School brought some further developments to backpack design. American children in particular were, during the 1940s, encouraged to use various backpack styles in which to carry their heavy loads of books, which until then were carted to class solely by means of leather straps.

War brought advances in backpack design too: the US Army issued its first rucksack in 1941, a canvas sack mounted on a steel-wire or rattan frame, with felt pads to protect the back, and side pockets with brass snap hooks. But clearly a successful design required specialist input. When the US War Department presented the rucksack to the National Ski Association's Winter Equipment Committee for review, it was promptly panned. Twelve improvements were recommended to the first model, which was quickly withdrawn from service. The 1942 version's greatest leap was in attaching the shoulder straps directly to the frame, which allowed for a much closer and more comfortable fit to the body. A tubular steel-framed version was also created in limited numbers.

It was not until 1952, with hiking now a fast-growing leisure pursuit, that outdoorsy Californian couple Asher and Nena Kelty introduced the next stage in backpack design. This incorporated a lightweight aluminium frame, with a support that helped distribute the weight off the shoulders and on to the hips, and is recognizable as something close to the styles worn on the first successful climbs of Everest in the 1950s. Far from allowing them to escape into the wilderness, however, the success of their backpack meant that the Keltys spent many long hours constructing their first commercial models from their garage.

Below: A rambler rests to check his map, 1930s.
Opposite: A member of the Overseas Contingent of the National Fire Service – non-combatants during World War II, but still requiring a rucksack to carry a full load of equipment.

THE
SATCHEL

'And then the whining school-boy, with his satchel / And shining morning face, creeping like snail / Unwillingly to school.' William Shakespeare's association of the satchel with school days in *As You Like It* (1599) is a strong one. In the 1950s, some 350 years later, schoolboys and girls were still using a brown leather satchel - distinguished by a panel on the front into which could be slotted a card bearing the owner's name - to carry both their books and the heavier weight of their disgruntlement to school.

But the satchel - if considered as a simple leather sack with a fold-over top and some form of shoulder strap - has had a longer history as a bag carried just as much by grown-ups. Roman legionnaires used what amounted to a basic leather satchel - they called it, sweetly, a *loculus*, or 'little place' - in which to carry their personal belongings. In the period AD 300 to 900, the satchel is said to have played a part in the conversion of some territories - including Scotland - to Christianity since satchels allowed the safe and protected carrying of religious texts by missionaries. 'Satchel' itself is a word with fourteenth-century Old English origins in *sacc*, and Old French *sachel*, meaning 'bag'.

It was not, however, until the late nineteenth century that the satchel became a prominent form of bag, thanks largely to the development of mail delivery services, when postmen would use an outsized satchel style in which to carry mail door to door. The US Postal Service, for example, used satchels from the 1860s, as did the riders of the Pony Express, preferring those in leather despite the additional weight. When the existing supply of leather post bags ran out in the early 1970s, the service replaced them with versions in canvas, which weighed half as much but had a working lifespan a quarter that of the leather variant.

Postal services also led to the origin of the similar messenger bag, as favoured by bicycle couriers, even if this was originally designed during the 1950s by tent manufacturer De Martini Globe Canvas Company to allow telephone and utility linesmen to carry heavy tools to the top of utility or telegraph poles. From the 1970s the same bags, made in canvas, were sold to New York City messenger services, who colour-coded them by firm and issued them to riders in exchange for a deposit. In 1980 mountaineer John Peters redesigned what came to be called the messenger bag to make it more functional specifically for bicycle couriers, using a tough technical nylon fabric for straps and the main body of the bag, adding also waterproof lining and reflective stripes. In 1983 he introduced the use of ballistic nylon.

The second half of the twentieth century brought a steady increase in the number of personal belongings individuals carried about their person or to and from work, driving interest in just such functional bag styles. Louis Armstrong won his nickname Satchmo as an abbreviation of 'satchel mouth', a consequence of his mouth's being said to be rather capacious. Small wonder too that the satchel has made regular appearances throughout popular film culture, helping it to become the definitive form of the basic, everyman bag - from Chewbacca's satchel in the *Star Wars* series to the British Army Mk VII gas bag of World War II carried (anachronistically) by Indiana Jones in *Raiders of the Lost Ark* (1981) and the various styles that appeared throughout the series of Harry Potter films. As Zach Galifianakis makes clear of his suspiciously small bag in *The Hangover* (2009): 'It's not a purse, it's a satchel.'

Above: Schoolboys on a street corner, Germany, 1928.
Below: An Austrian postman, c.1870, complete with trusty satchel.
Opposite: Chewbacca, clothed only in fur and so without pockets - and in need of a satchel, in *Star Wars: Episode V, The Empire Strikes Back* (1980).

8.
GROOMING

POMADE / THE BEARD / TATTOOS

POMADE

Hairstyles for men have changed as radically over the centuries as have fashions in clothing – long, short, pony-tailed, permed, shaven and bewigged, through to side-swept bangs and the so-called fauxhawk. But it is only since the 1800s that men have sought to use unguents as a means of controlling and styling their hair, with bear fat being the early, unappealing main ingredient – one popular early nineteenth-century brand was James Atkinson's Bears Grease. This was later replaced with, though only slightly improved by, lard, as well as with beeswax and petroleum jelly. As the Brylcreem ad of the 1950s aptly put it, 'a little dab'll do ya'.

It was the 1920s that saw the first real explosion in options. Brylcreem – created by the Birmingham County Chemical Company in Britain in 1928 and first sold as Elite Hair Dressing Cream – may have been one of the most famous names on the chemist's shelf, but it was certainly not alone. Murray's (with its Nu Nile or orange-canned Superior Pomade), Morgan's, Black & White, Sweet Georgia Brown and Royal Crown, all launched between 1925 and 1936, were also household names in their respective home countries. Dax was a popular later name. The use of such products was widespread in an era in which a man's hair, when not covered by a hat, was expected to be shiny, dark and ordered. Such a style was central to the time's idea of what it was to be a debonair man.

One long-running TV advertisement for Brylcreem, aired in the United States during the 1950s, showed a chance encounter between a man and a woman while at a zoo, setting the stage for romance. 'But then he had to take off his hat and, uh-oh, poor guy,' the narrator says, as the woman looks aghast at the sight. 'Dry, lifeless hair can take the fun out of life. But you can put it back with Brylcreem. Brylcreem gives your hair that look the ladies love: excitingly clean, disturbingly healthy, so masculine…'

In helping men sculpt their hair, pomade – the ancestor of modern-day gels, oils, tonics and pastes – also made possible distinctive hairstyles, which in turn helped to define style-led subcultures. The rock and roll aesthetic of the mid-1950s, pioneered by such singers as Bill Hayley & His Comets and Elvis Presley, was at least in part identified by Hayley's kiss curl and Presley's wet-look pompadour. The DA, or duck's arse, was made possible by pomade – in this style long hair was slicked to the back of the head to create a ridge or fin, as favoured by the British youth subculture the Teddy boys and representing one of their nods to Americana.

Rockers and greasers, the British biker clans of the 1950s, also saw greased hair as a central pillar of their style, especially given its direct contrast with the hairstyles of their arch-rivals, the mods. The mods' clean 'college boy' hair cuts – a Perry Como, perhaps, after the American singer, or, at its most extravagant, the bouncy bouffant of a back-combed style, both often acquired at ladies' hair salons rather than at the traditional men's barbers – were almost ostentatiously free of pomade.

During World War II a small tub of Brylcreem was issued to all British servicemen as part of their personal care kits, and flyers in the RAF were dubbed the 'Brylcreem Boys' for their spic-and-span, short back and sides haircuts. After the restrictions in hairstyles imposed by army conscription during the war, many men chose to grow their hair somewhat longer. Pomades allowed hair to be a means of self-expression, or a mark of belonging to a perhaps rather outré clan even if one was attired in overalls or a suit for work. Not that it would last, though: the 1960s saw the advent of a new libertinism in dress that encouraged the styles of the Beatles and other 'long-haired hippies', as they might be disparagingly referred to, to dispense with any kind of tonsorial control.

Above: Murray's Superior Hair Dressing Pomade – in a tin pot reminiscent of the typical packaging of the 1940s and 1950s.
Below: This 1954 advertisement features a man applying Brylcreem pomade with a pair of brushes – dexterity required.

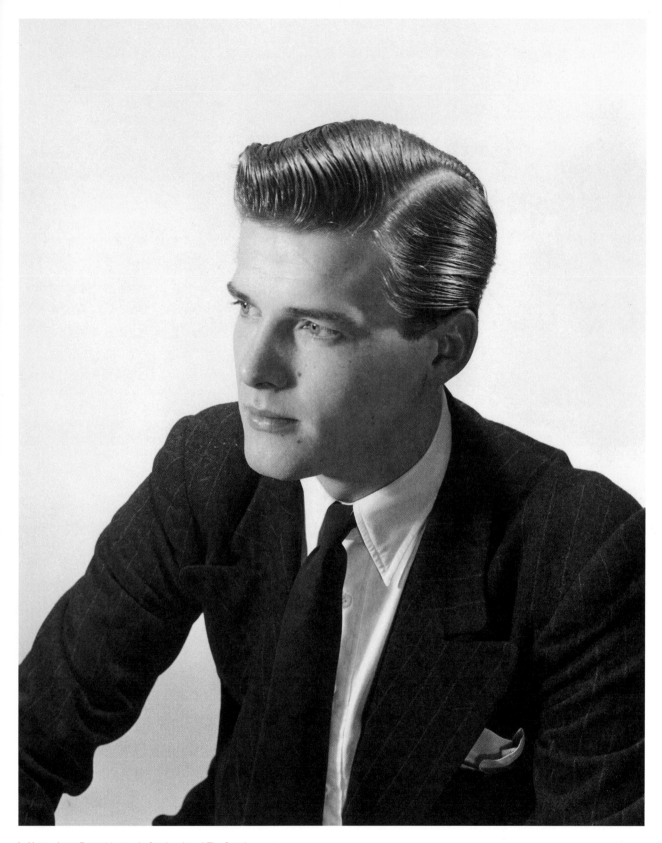

Above: Actor Roger Moore – before he played 'The Saint' or James Bond – models for a hair grooming product advertisement.

THE
BEARD

The beard, like hair, has long been a subject both of fashion and of societal constraint. The beard may have symbolized wisdom – as the look of Socrates, 'the bearded master', was said to suggest – but it also had a certain barbarous or outsider quality, as evoked by the beards worn by the Vikings, the hippies of the 1960s, the biker gangs of the 1970s, the members of rock band ZZ Top and, in the twenty-first century, the hipsters of New York and London. And these connotations stand quite apart from the religious, political and sexual affiliations that facial hair have also signified.

Archaeological evidence exists to suggest that men began to remove their facial hair as long ago as 100,000 BC – by plucking rather than shaving, since a sharp enough edge would not be developed until the Bronze Age. It was the ancient Greeks who first loaded the wearing of a beard with significance other than being a primary characteristic of masculinity and virility (an association noted by psychological studies since: *Philosophy of Beards*, published in 1880, observed that 'the absence of beard is usually a sign of physical and moral weakness'). The Greeks, rather, conceived of it as suggesting certain sage qualities, as did ancient Indian and Middle Eastern cultures, where the public shaving of a beard was deemed a kind of punishment. The beard's suggestion of manliness was further undermined by Alexander the Great, who in 323 BC is said to have instructed all of his soldiers to go clean-shaven, for the practical reason that the beard offered an enemy a dangerous purchase during hand-to-hand combat.

More than two millennia later, the prohibition against wearing a beard in military service remained for the armies of many countries, notably those of the United States, which have particularly strict rules against facial hair. Historically there have been exceptions: submariners, for example, were typically permitted to wear a 'patrol beard', since water supplies were so limited that their use for shaving made little sense, while special units such as the sappers of the French Foreign Legion have worn beards as a mark

Below left: Karl Marx – philosopher, economist, revolutionary and beard-wearer.
Below right: Spanish surrealist Salvador Dalí.

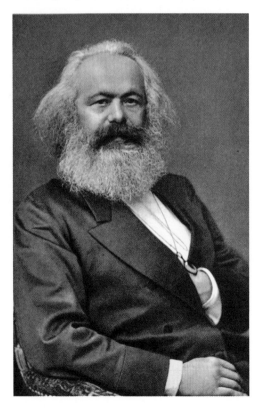

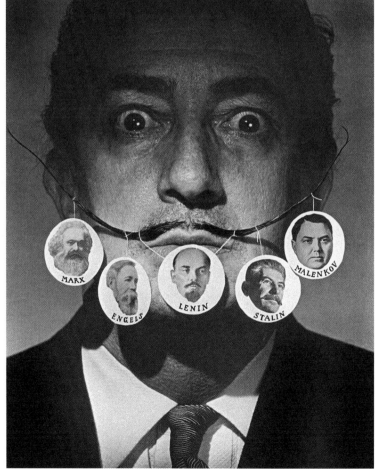

of their distinction. Often moustaches and sideburns have been permitted, although not in the Royal Navy – which has, however, allowed beards. In some instances some kind of facial hair has even been a requirement. After the Crimean War all ranks of soldiers in the British Army were prohibited from shaving above the top lip, a prohibition that technically remained in place until 1916, when Lieutenant-General Nevil Macready – who was known to hate his own moustache – gladly abolished it.

Indeed, the prevalence, or not, of the beard over the centuries has often been a product less of fashion than of direction by authority. Despite the beard having been associated with both godliness and kingliness for millennia (female pharaohs even wore a postiche, a false beard made of gold), King Henry VIII of England taxed wearers of beards in 1535, even though he wore a beard himself. Elizabeth I taxed them too, based on the age and social class of the wearer. Peter I of Russia directed courtiers and officials to go clean-shaven in 1698, similarly taxing those who wished to keep them – and making them wear a medal declaring that 'beards are a ridiculous ornament'. Even in times when facial hair became a purely personal choice, notably after the availability of affordable, effective razors at the turn of the twentieth century, social opprobrium was a powerful force: Abraham Lincoln, the first fully bearded American president, was accused of 'putting on airs' when he grew his after he had won office.

Wearing the more sculpted facial hair styles of the later nineteenth and twentieth centuries was to invite the same uncertain reading by some onlookers, be it goatee or mutton chops, chin strap, chin curtain or soul patch. Across the many styles of beard – from Charles Darwin's long white beard to Karl Marx's full Santa Claus effect – and similarly across different approaches to the moustache – from Wyatt Earp's handlebar style to Salvador Dalí's greased wire-like version and baseball star Rollie Fingers's impressive curls – a definitive style of 'face furniture' has always made some kind of statement, although not necessarily one under the wearer's control.

Below left: Novelist Ernest Hemingway at the desk in Malaga, Spain, where he wrote *The Dangerous Summer*.
Below right: Animation film-maker Liu Jian, in Nanjing in 2014.

TATTOOS

For some, the tattoo remains associated with thuggery and the working class, with base tastes and rough edges, closely tied up as it is with the unsettling idea of somehow desecrating one's body. But for a growing number of others 'body art', as it is now widely referred to, has lost these negative connotations. Tattoos are no longer the stereotypical preserve of the nationalist (the flag, the British bulldog), the merchant seaman (the anchor, the mermaid), the soldier (battle commemorations or the girl back home), the 'Ride to Live' biker, the gang member or the criminal ('love' and 'hate' across the knuckles, or what is in tattoo circles called a tear – a dot near the eye that represents a sentence served). By the end of the twentieth century tattoos had become increasingly common across gender, class, profession and age.

The tattoo rehabilitation was rapid too: until 1997 New York, for example, had a city-wide ban on tattooing. Not that this was the first time state authorities had attempted to clamp down on tattooing. The ancient Greeks and Romans had used tattooing to mark spies, slaves and prisoners: with the advent of Christianity, a backlash against the practice began. Constantine, the first Christian Roman emperor, banned facial tattooing in AD 325 because it was believed to be an affront to God's image. In 787 Pope Adrian I banned tattooing entirely.

Tattooing is believed to date to prehistoric times; the 5,000-year-old body of a man preserved in the ice and uncovered in the Alps during the 1990s was found to have a number of tattoos. Two female Egyptian mummies, a priestess and a dancer, dating to 2160 BC, were also tattooed. The ancient Europeans, notably the Picts and the Britons, also had a strong tattoo tradition. To these ancient peoples tattoos represented not defilement but order.

Tattooing was a prominent art form around the world, from Hawaii and Samoa to the Maoris of New Zealand, with their elaborate facial tattoos, and from the Mojave, Cree and Arapaho tribes of North America to the Aztec and Inca of South America. In Japan tattooing was nothing short of a national craze during the Edo period from 1600 to 1868. In Europe, a new consideration of tattooing was sparked by the voyages of British explorer and navigator Captain James Cook to the South Pacific in the second half of the eighteenth century. Many members of his crew returned from Polynesia with tattoos, and indeed the word itself derives from the Polynesian *tatau*.

Opposite: Robert de Niro in the remake of *Cape Fear* (1991).
Below left: A tattooed biker in New Orleans in 1978 – his tattoo marks him out as an outlaw 'One Percenter', tougher than the 99 per cent who live within the 'system'.
Below right: Vertigo-free workmen high over New York, building the Rockefeller Centre in 1935.

Skin markings were likely to have been made accidentally at first by the rubbing of soot into a cut, a process then mimicked deliberately using a sharp implement and vegetable dye. This was the basic manner of tattooing until the American tattoo artist Samuel O'Reilly patented the electric rotary tattoo machine in 1891, the forerunner of the modern tattoo machine, which injects ink under the skin using a rapidly moving needle (a technique copied by prisoners using wire, a disposable pen and a cassette-player motor).

The tattoo was typically a statement of membership among traditional working-class tribes. Tattoos symbolized manliness or danger, a visual shorthand that Hollywood and the advertising industry tapped into, as with Robert de Niro's character in the 1991 remake of *Cape Fear*, or tobacco company Phillip Morris's creation in 1955 of the Marlboro Man, complete with tattoo on the back of his hand, to reposition Marlboro cigarettes as a masculine brand.

Yet privately, and counter to the tattoo's usual image, the well-to-do have never been strangers to the ink. Countless aristocratic holy crusaders were marked for life, as were King Harold II of England, Prince Albert, King George V of Britain and Tsar Nicholas II of Russia. Perhaps this was another example of a pattern of appropriation of working-class characteristics by the middle and upper classes, in much the same way that having a suntan, once the mark of those who had to work outside, became symbolic of wealth and leisure.

Tattoos have also been used for identification purposes. When the baby of famous aviator Charles Lindbergh was kidnapped in 1932, many worried American parents had their children tattooed, while the introduction of social security numbers in the United States in 1936 prompted a rush to have those tattooed on the skin too. Although the inter-war years made a tattoo de rigueur for servicemen, the Nazi practice of forcibly tattooing Jews in the concentration camps was in part responsible for a tattoo slump after World War II.

It was not until the cultural revolution of the 1960s and 1970s that tattooing slowly began to achieve art status, largely through the opening of trade between the USA and Japan and the introduction of more refined, less countercultural designs, which were publicly adopted by, for example, Janis Joplin, Cher and Peter Fonda. It is that artistic element of tattooing that has given it such a presence throughout history: tattoos are permanent but the medium is flexible enough to embrace new forms and imagery.

Latterly tattoos have become statements of membership in newer tribes, such as ecological, New Age spiritual, activist – even corporate, with employees of Nike, as one alleged tradition has it, having the Nike Swoosh tattooed on their upper thigh. It may be seen as a form of personal branding.

Below: A skinhead, photographed at the Rebellion Festival weekend, Blackpool, UK, in 2011.
Opposite: A mix of references are worn by this tattooed attendee of the Wilderness Festival in Oxfordshire, UK, in 2013.

9.
ACCESSORIES

BRACES / THE TIE / THE POCKET SQUARE / GLOVES / THE BELT / THE WALLET

BRACES

Braces, or suspenders as they are known in the United States, were once considered to be part of a gentleman's underwear. Dress etiquette dictated that they should not be seen. This was not an issue during times when the three-piece suit (or a sleeveless pullover) was standard fare, but it could be a problem in hot weather. Indeed, it may have been during a series of heatwaves across western Europe in the 1890s that men first replaced braces with belt: doing so allowed them to remove their waistcoats without fear of social opprobrium. Keeping one's braces covered was considered necessary at least up until World War II; in 1938 a town on Long Island, New York, tried to ban men from wearing braces without a coat, calling it 'sartorial indecency'.

The story of braces has, from the twentieth century at least, been one of the battle between braces and belt as a means of keeping one's trousers up. Tailors have long insisted that the better-dressed man will wear his suit with braces, since these allow trouser pleats, if present, to open up and high-waisted trousers to hang better over the shoe. In fact, some will advise that trousers be worn slightly looser than necessary so that they literally hang from one's braces. Meanwhile, poorer families, for whom hand-me-down trousers might be commonplace, found braces an easy means of ensuring one size fitted all.

Certainly, button-on braces were considered such an essential part of the well-dressed man's attire that few trousers at all came with belt loops until the 1920s, when styles began to move down from the natural waist, and when war with Germany was declared in 1939, the actor Ralph Richardson went immediately to his tailors to order six pairs of braces lest the imminent rationing of fabric might leave them in short supply. Levi's stopped putting suspender buttons on its jeans around 1937, replacing them with belt loops. By then the convenience, simplicity, practicality and perhaps more everyman quality of the belt had begun to make it the more popular choice.

The invention of braces is attributed to the French, who from revolutionary times wore *bretelles*, strips of ribbon fixed into trouser buttonholes. The idea spread across the Channel to Britain, where the new dark and neat menswear pioneered by dandy George 'Beau' Brummell saw the wide uptake of silk or satin braces as a means of keeping one's closely fitted trousers wrinkle-free.

Opposite: Michael Douglas as Gordon Gekko in *Wall Street* (1987), the seminal tale of corporate greed.
Above: A 1906 advertisement for Bull Dog Suspenders from Boston's Hewes & Potter.
Below: Men stroll through Paris, their braces on show during a 1928 heatwave.

In 1820 Britain's first specialist maker of braces, Albert Thurston, opened for business on London's Panton Street. Many competitors followed, each vying for dominance by emphasizing their quality materials, but also their newfangled inventiveness: one company, British Argosy, sold its strong but lightweight braces as being 'most suitable for summer wear'. Fashion also played its part: in the 1850s H-shaped-back braces were the most popular, but these would give way to the X-shape and eventually the Y-shape; while soberly dressed men could privately revel in the variety of cloths, colours and patterns braces afforded. In the 1920s some doctors recommended the rigours of wearing braces as a means of combating big bellies, which, they argued, belts only accommodated.

In the United States, from 1736 Benjamin Franklin popularized the wearing of 'gallowses', as braces were sometimes called, and insisted they be worn by the men of the first voluntary fire service, in Philadelphia, which he founded. American firemen still wear braces today, typically in red. In 1871 one of the first patents for braces, or rather for a similar, supposedly more comfortable alternative to them – 'adjustable and detachable straps for garments' – was issued to one Samuel Clemens, better known as Mark Twain. The first patent for metal clip-on braces was issued to a David Roth in 1894, although it took another century for a non-slip clip to be patented.

It was not invention, however, so much as fad that allowed braces to resurface periodically over the latter half of the twentieth century, albeit peaking in very different worlds. Braces became part of the uniform of the skinheads, the much-maligned British style tribe of the late 1960s to the early 1980s, who sometimes wore colour-coded elasticated braces as a totem of allegiance to a traditional British working-class heritage and aesthetic. They wore them with button-down shirts and rolled-up Levi's 501 jeans, without braces buttons, which meant that clip-ons were the order of the day – typically narrow and sometimes worn loose around the waist. In 1987 Gordon Gekko, the anti-hero of Oliver Stone's *Wall Street*, kick-started a fashion for braces (in particular red ones) as symbolic of the power, success and excess among banking's 'masters of the universe'. The look was then worn with less loaded connotations as the signature style of the veteran US broadcaster Larry King.

Above: Albert Einstein at home in Princeton, New Jersey, in 1947.
Opposite: Skinheads, without shirts, with braces, at a Bad Manners gig in the UK in 1980.

THE TIE

For some the tie is something of a mystery in the twenty-first century: just what is it for? It serves no functional purpose, other than perhaps to 'finish' an ensemble or, in certain settings, to meet societal expectations. Playing against this notion of conformity is the suggestion that the tie might be an opportunity for personal expression.

That certainly was not its original intention. Some form of neckwear has been worn for millennia. Characters on Trajan's Column (AD 113) in Rome are said to show the earliest recorded example of neckwear in art – something akin to the scarf-like *focale* worn by Roman legionnaires – although the soldiers of the Terracotta Army (dating to c. 210 BC) of the Qin Dynasty wore a silk cord around their necks, probably as a symbol of status.

It was not until the sixteenth century, though, that something resembling the modern, decorative tie was worn. Croatian mercenaries for the French army during the Thirty Years' War (1618–48) wore a cravat-like tie – 'cravat' possibly being a linguistic mangling of 'Croat', and by then a word already used in Italy – ostensibly as a means of signalling their comradeship. It took King Louis XIV, King of France until 1715, to adopt the style and give it credibility in civilian society. It was from this that a simple scarf, perhaps of flax and trimmed in lace, began its evolution: first as a garment worn tied around the neck many times, leaving just short ends on show – and providing genuine protection against the cold – towards silk neck bands knotted in a bow (the obvious forerunner of the bow-tie), and finally arriving at a variation in which the cloth was knotted so as to leave the ends long. Ideal, as the early nickname had it, as a 'soup catcher', sometimes requiring a tie-clip to keep it out of one's starter.

During the eighteenth and nineteenth centuries, the codification of the tie was more intricate. Choosing a knot was considered such a statement of self-determination that even Louis XIV, a man used to being physically dressed by manservants, is said to have insisted on knotting his own tie (or rather the neckwear that then passed as such). George 'Beau' Brummell, the hugely influential early nineteenth-century English dandy, would knot his tie just so, working through a pile of the starched linens then worn as ties until he was properly satisfied. As the *Journal des Dames* noted in 1835, '*La cravate, c'est l'homme*'. A knot, indeed, was a mark of community. The four-in-hand knot, named after the knot used in reins to control a four-horse rig, was said to have been used by members of the Four-in-Hand Club in London; the same knot was known as the *regate* in France, since there it was associated with yachtsmen. Either way, sport is likely to have been the origin of this particularly secure knot, since sportsmen – obliged to wear a tie even during competition – needed their knots to stay knotted.

Opposite: Cary Grant in his dressing room in 1955.
Above: Henry Fonda in an early studio portrait, taken in 1945.
Below: King George VI, British monarch from 1936–52 and known as the 'Dandy Monarch', here in 1936.

Above: Fred Astaire demonstrates not only his leap but
also the signature way in which he wears a tie as a belt.
Bing Crosby looks on.
Opposite: Rapper Sean Combs at a catwalk show in 2001.

It is to the modern era that the tie as it is now known dates. In 1924, American tailor Jesse Langsdorf patented an 'all-weather, wrinkle-free' design whose attributes are characteristic of most neckties in Western dress today: three pieces of cloth, stitched and folded into a point and, most pertinently, with the fabric cut on the bias (at a 45-degree angle to the fibres of the material), allowing the tie to be knotted and untied without leaving creases in it. The fabric, too, grew louder and more expressive.

Yet this bolder tie actually derives from institutions not commonly associated – at least, not in the modern era – with flamboyance. The British private school had popularized the wearing of a striped tie to denote membership; in 1880 students of Exeter College, Oxford University, began donning the ribbons from their straw boaters as a form of neckwear. Ties made in college colours soon followed. Gentlemen's private clubs similarly adopted their own ties. Anecdotally at least, this tradition was first prompted by a joke. The actor Norman Forbes-Robertson, a prominent member of London's esteemed thespian club the Garrick, wore a pale pink and green tie to lunch one day and, on being asked of its origin, quipped that it was the official club tie. Soon after, it was adopted as such.

In the 1920s, regimental ties – striped in regimental colours – were widely adopted by British armed forces personnel at functions requiring civilian dress. The wearing of a tie representing a regiment (or, indeed, any institution) to which you did not actually belong was considered a serious breach of etiquette, if not a disciplinary matter. Not so in the United States, however. There the influential men's outfitters Brooks Brothers took the style and made it a menswear standard, with one alteration: while on regimental ties the stripes ran from the left shoulder down to the right, Brooks Brothers' ran from the right down to the left. The so-called 'rep' tie, after the weave of silk used in its construction, soon became an Ivy League style fixture.

Nor were colour and pattern the only means of making your tie talk. Knot types in the twentieth century included the likes of the English, favoured by King Edward VIII before he invented his own Windsor knot (very similar to that worn by his father, George V), and known in Italy as the *scappino*; the half-Windsor; the diagonal, which leaves a fold in sight right across the knot; and the American, favoured by presidents Nixon, Ford and Carter as best suiting the then fashion for wider ties.

Width came in and out of fashion over the period too. It had been the chief characteristic of ties of the early half of the century: with the rise of the dark and sober suit, ties were designed to offer a splash of colour at the neck and were not worn long enough to touch the trouser top. In the 1960s tie styles fluctuated from bootlace-thin to the wide look pioneered by Michael Fish, founder in 1966 of influential Savile Row tailors Mr Fish. Punning on his name, these would come to be called kipper ties.

THE POCKET SQUARE

For such an apparently insignificant piece of fabric, the dress handkerchief, pochette or pocket square is loaded with myriad options for self-expression. Business types might prefer the simple so-called presidential or pesko style – folded at right angles to present a neat 1-centimetre (half-inch) ridge of colour above the jacket pocket, a look that is very Sean Connery-era James Bond. Then there is the one-, two- or three-point fold, like a mountain range rising from your breast pocket. Clark Gable preferred the exactitude of the single sharp triangle of fabric, conscious perhaps of the tailor's complaint that anything other than a hard press and precision fold may ruin the line of the jacket.

Other styles include the puff, reverse puff, winged puff and diagonal shell, not to mention the advanced origami of the Cagney (named after James Cagney), with its multiple, multidirectional peaks – a style perhaps not so readily pulled out to give to a lady in distress. Conversely, there is the more flamboyant, bohemian style made popular by Fred Astaire, which involved essentially stuffing an unfolded silk handkerchief from its centre straight into the pocket, leaving a floral spray effect. Film director Alfred Hitchcock even used the folding of a pocket square to reflect its owner's state of mind, in *Secret Agent* (1936), for example, contrasting the mania of Peter Lorre's character – wearing an outsize, flamboyant pocket square – to that of the repressed and regimented mindset of John Gielgud's, his pocket square remaining neat and pristine.

However one wore it, by the early 1900s the pocket square had become a dash of colourful or patterned cotton, linen or silk that was an essential finishing touch to one's attire and, depending on your sartorial esprit, either complemented or contrasted with your tie (but never matched it). It had, in other words, made the transition from something with which one mopped one's sweaty brow or blew one's nose – and thus, etiquette dictated, was kept tucked away in one's trouser pockets – to an accessory for purposes of display. The carrying of two handkerchiefs became commonplace, one as an accent of colour in one's outfit, the other as a practical if perhaps unhygienic piece of cloth (later superseded for some men by disposable paper tissues such as those introduced by Kleenex in 1924).

Above: Jazz trumpeter Louis Armstrong wipes his face with his handkerchief.
Right: Cary Grant, posing for a studio portrait during the 1930s.

Given its basic nature and essential functionality, the pocket square's ancestor, the handkerchief, had, of course, been an object of personal style for centuries before, and of ceremony for millennia. The wealthy of ancient Egypt might carry a handkerchief in white linen for use and one expensively dyed with red oxide power (which would rapidly fade if ever washed) for show; gladiatorial games in Rome would be started by the symbolic dropping of an *orarium*, a fabric square, with the Emperor Aurelian in AD 271 issuing handkerchiefs for spectators to wave as a sign of their appreciation.

By the Middle Ages the expense of the fine fabric and costliness of dyeing processes meant that the handkerchief for display remained the preserve of the well-off. Courtly knights, for example, carried them to express their having a certain lady's favour; King Richard II was an enthusiastic fourteenth-century exponent of their use in the English court (although predominantly to cover his nose with); while the display of handkerchiefs in the Renaissance became a heavily codified form of communication, especially in matters of love and lust.

The fashionableness of the handkerchief was further driven by royal approval, with the court of King Louis XVI of France encouraging the carrying of examples made of the rarest fabrics, finely and opulently worked. These were doused in perfume and held to the nose to mask unpleasant odours, whether of the street or of one's infrequently washed companions. This in turn led to the affectation of displaying the handkerchief. Apocryphal though the story may be, Marie Antoinette is said to have insisted that the runaway trend for ever larger, more showy handkerchiefs was making them impractical as fashionable accessories, leading Louis to proclaim that handkerchiefs should be both roughly 40 x 40 centimetres (16 x 16 inches) in size and, just as importantly, square. In this way Marie Antoinette started a small revolution in style, before helping to prompt a much more significant one in politics.

Right: George Sanders, in the typically wide-shouldered tailoring of the late 1940s and early 1950s.

GLOVES

Although gloves have been worn by men and women alike since at least the time of the ancient Greeks, while women have historically donned them as displays of status or out of decorum, men have worn them for action – or at least to imply it. In more knightly times, a man might quite literally throw down a gauntlet before someone from whom he had received some offence and from whom he was demanding 'satisfaction': this was usually a presage to some form of duel. The offender might respond with his glove too, by slapping his opponent-to-be across the face with it. This action – more a symbolic gesture than anything designed to injure – was a way of accepting the challenge, as any knight was duty-bound to do in order to protect his honour. To receive a glove from a woman, however, meant something else entirely: it was a sign of favour, such that a knight might wear the glove in a small bag around his neck.

Jump forward some 700 years and the knight's steed would become motorized and the glove would be dubbed the 'motor gauntlet'. The driving glove charted the evolution of the car, from the unheated, open-topped vehicle requiring heavyweight wool-lined leather protection for the hands, through to the later versions that, in some macho minds, necessitated a specialist glove, palmed in thin deer or lambskin for better grip of the wheel, with a mesh or cut-away backing to keep the hands cool, and sometimes even fingerless.

The gloves made for easier turning of the large wooden steering wheels standard in the early days of motoring, and were an accessory that largely fell from fashion in the 1960s when car manufacturers began both to use smaller steering wheels and to apply a non-slip surface to them. That, however, did not stop driving gloves from retaining an air of caddish, cat burglar or playboy chic about them: Steve McQueen wears his in powder blue, to match his tie, in *The Thomas Crowne Affair* (1968), for example. 'Handle with driving gloves', as one 1970 magazine ad for the Chevrolet Corvette put it, adding that this was a vehicle though that did not need to be handled with kid gloves. One kept one's driving gloves, of course, in the car's glove compartment, for which it was so named.

Below: Steve McQueen in a still from *The Thomas Crowne Affair* (1968), driving gloves on – just the kind one might select from this 1970 ad (shown below right).

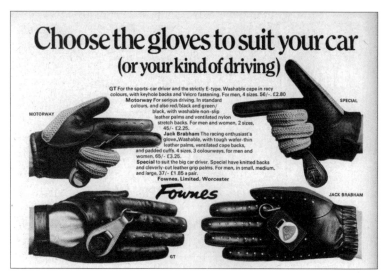

Unlike gloves for women – which have been subject to fashion since the twelfth century, when the glove as recognized today first began to be made – gloves for men have always been functional first and foremost, even if that function was perhaps to express one's high status rather than keep one's hands warm. Henry II of England was buried wearing gloves in 1189, as were King John in 1216 and King Edward I in 1307. A gentleman might be more inclined to carry his gloves than actually wear them, which explains why gloves of the Renaissance period especially could be so wide – it made them easier to hold. During the Regency period in Britain (1811–20) the reverse applied: a man of rank would have a variety of pairs and know that it would be considered a poor show to be seen in public without a pair on.

Inevitably, a complex glove etiquette evolved: one never shook another man's hand wearing a glove, for example. A nineteenth-century guide to gentlemanly dressing insisted that a man of class would change his gloves six times a day; brown, black and navy blue were popular colours, as was yellow, while white gloves would be worn for evening wear.

This glove wardrobe was, at least, much more feasible after the invention by James Winter in 1807 (the year rubber gloves were also first patented) of the so-called gloving donkey, a machine for sewing gloves that greatly reduced the price of what until then had been a skilfully hand-crafted product. Furthermore, French master glove-maker Xavier Jouvin, who worked during the first half of the nineteenth century, introduced the idea of glove sizing, providing the first reliable fits; this in turn had been made possible by the development of high-grade steel, which meant that knives for cutting glove leather uniformly could be made.

The more mass-produced gloves were, however, the less symbolic they became. Indeed, perhaps the last time they were treated as such – Michael Jackson's Swarovski crystal-covered glove aside – was at the Mexico City Summer Olympics of 1968, when African-American athletes John Carlos and Tommie Smith took to the podium to receive their medals and each raised a single, black-leather-gloved fist as a salute to Black Power and the human rights movement.

THE BELT

In 1937 Levi's finally saw that the tide had turned. Until then its jeans had come with suspender buttons and a back cinch buckle. Then the company added belt loops, as the preference for wearing belts grew, the idea being that if the wearer opted for a belt, he could remove the back cinch himself. By the mid-1920s it was already becoming clear that this was what the vast majority of their customers – younger ones especially – were doing. The belt, and by extension the belt loop, had taken over: one could even find belt loops on baseball uniforms. The suspender buttons and cinch were removed from Levi's designs altogether.

Until this period a man would typically use braces and buttons to hold up his trousers (although well into the 1930s labourers, not wishing to feel constricted by braces, might simply run a belt around the top of their high-rise trousers whether they had loops or not). Belts were principally worn to hang things from (a function dating back to the Bronze Age), used especially by those who carried a sword or, later, a sidearm.

Superstitions abounded as to the mystical qualities in battle of the stones that might decorate a belt, and such was the symbolism of the belt that to seize an enemy's belt was in some sense to have defeated him, much as one army might seek to seize the other's flag. The belt might be said to have continued this militaristic association in martial arts and boxing, in which belts are a marker of a practitioner's achievement. Conversely, in the nineteenth century, for some – admittedly widely ridiculed – soldiers, those of the Russian army in particular, wide belts were worn as a kind of corset, to nip in the waist and achieve the silhouette and posture then considered fashionably officer-like.

If the belt itself offered little opportunity for self-expression, the buckle did. The first belts were simply tied, although what amounts to a form of fastening made from bone or antler horn has been ascribed to prehistoric peoples. It was with the ability to work metal that the Romans first formed purpose-made buckles, in iron, and later in bronze. By around the fifth century, most belts would come with a buckle, which opened up the decorative possibilities of shaping, stamping, engraving and gem-setting. Such costly processes signified the wearer's wealth and position and, later, his occupation. The Sutton Hoo burial hoard of Anglo-Saxon (sixth- to seventh-century) treasures uncovered in the UK in 1939 included an extremely elaborate carved gold belt buckle.

Although more outlandish buckle designs are often associated with the cowboys of the American Wild West, the fact is that the original pioneers and frontiersmen would have worn suspenders. It was only in the early twentieth century that western, Native Indian and rodeo-influenced plate buckle designs took hold – including the traditional Navajo combination of silver and turquoise; eagles or longhorn cattle; and the Stars and Stripes – by which time the public image of the cowboy was already becoming the stuff of mythology. This, of course, was enhanced further by Hollywood's golden era of westerns from the 1930s to 1960s. For *Red River* (1948) director Howard Hawks gave John Wayne and other cast members belts with a silver buckle depicting the Red River ranch's cattle brand, a D with two wavy lines; years later Wayne made a return gift of a buckle to Hawks.

This glossier cowboy image is what would come to inform the dress of some country and western singers and – in wildly exaggerated form – the white rhinestone-covered jumpsuit style worn by Elvis Presley for performances through the 1970s.

Above: A Uraguayan gaucho's elaborate belt – complete with silver horseshoe buckle and several pockets for money, papers and knife.
Below: Singer Jermaine Jackson, of the Jackson 5, in 1972.

Above: Clint Eastwood and Eric Fleming pose for a portrait on the set of 1960s TV series *Rawhide*.

THE WALLET

The story of the wallet encompasses the story of currency. A type of wallet or pouch was carried in ancient Greece for keeping or transporting food rather than valuables. With the advent of metal coinage, around the 1300s, something was required to carry it in, especially since the pocket had yet to be invented (this would not happen until the late seventeenth century). Leather pouches, much the same as those used by the Greeks, were filled with coins and strung from a belt. They were then either kept out of sight, like a modern-day travel belt ('he that displays too often his wife and his wallet is in danger of having both of them borrowed,' as Benjamin Franklin would note), or worn as a kind of accessory, with the wealthy tending to wear purses heavily ornamented or decorated with fine embroidery. Towards the late fourteenth century the word 'wallet' first came into use, deriving from a Germanic word relating to 'well', with all that suggests of depth and sustenance – although at that point it referred to a bag for provisions, again like that of the Greeks.

In the late seventeenth century, paper currency came into use. A specially made form of container was required for this: something more akin to a small leather envelope-style folder was used, which protected the precious notes and was still typically worn attached to a belt. This was, however, something required by the very few. Indeed, given that as late as the mid-1800s most working-class men would earn so little as to easily be paid in coin, and coin that would disappear almost immediately on necessities, the wallet would soon became symbolic of personal wealth – the archetypal 'fat wallet'. Most men simply had no need for a billfold. Those who could use one typically operated by paying against a line of credit with tradespeople they knew in person, settling the account periodically.

In fact, it was only in the 1950s, with the introduction of charge and credit cards – first proposed and named in Edward Bellamy's sci-fi novel of 1887 *Looking Backward*, and pioneered by oil and airline companies as a means of payment by regular customers – that the wallet became anything more than a single space. The introduction of the earliest credit or charge cards – by Diners Club, American Express and Bank of America in the United States in the 1950s, and by Barclaycard in the UK in 1966 – required a new kind of wallet with dedicated slots and sections. The more cards a man had, the more he needed space in which to put them: the bi-fold wallet, which folded in two so as to be more readily stowed in a trouser pocket, became a tri-fold.

Wallet manufacturers were quick to sell their wallets as something special, referring, as one 1957 American advertisement had it, to their 'banker-style construction', or to their being an 'executive-style slim fold', or to a model's being available with matching 'pocket secretary' – essentially a small leather-bound perforated paper notepad with a slot containing a mechanical pencil. Other wallets came pressed with a metal motif – a golfer, sports car or locomotive perhaps – complete with matching keyring and cufflinks. Nor were makers slow to introduce novelty wallets: in 1952 one American manufacturer introduced what it called its 'Western styles', complete with Roy Rogers and Hopalong Cassidy models. The latter came with an image of the 'two-gun hero in color on both sides, lucky coin in secret pocket and "special agent's pass"'.

pick the billfold that's right for his type

ROLFS

Above: Sportsman, city gent or man about town, a 1950s advertisement for Rolfs suggests different wallets for different kinds of men.
Below: US actor Lon Chaney counts some cash from his wallet.

Above: The wallet is a place to store not only cash and documents but fond memories, as this promotional image from 1945 suggests.

10.
TOOLS

THE FOUNTAIN PEN / THE POCKET
KNIFE / SUNGLASSES / THE UMBRELLA /
SPECTACLES

THE FOUNTAIN PEN

Such is the perceived significance of signing using a fountain pen rather than a humble ballpoint that politicians and heads of state regularly use one to sign treaties, declarations, charters and international agreements of import. Soviet General Secretary Mikhail Gorbachev and US President Ronald Reagan used fountain pens to sign the Intermediate-Range Nuclear Forces Treaty of 1987, and General Douglas MacArthur used one to sign the Japanese surrender at the end of WWII.

One of the most famous fountain pens beloved by statesmen and others is the fat-barrelled Meisterstück by Montblanc, a status symbol that was carried by, among others, Ernest Hemingway, John F. Kennedy and the cinematic James Bond. With its nib engraved with '4810' – the height of Mont Blanc in metres – the Meisterstück, launched by the Simplo Filler Pen Company in 1924, is considered to be such an exemplar of the fountain pen and all it might suggest of an appreciation for craft and for the art of writing that it has a place in the permanent collection of New York's Museum of Modern Art.

Other classics of the form, such as the Pelikan 100 and Parker Duofold, have won their own admirers too. The Bauhaus designer László Moholy-Nagy is said to have favoured a Parker 51, designed by Marlin Baker in 1941 and with a barrel made from the same Lucite material as used to make the canopy of a Mustang fighter plane. Parker promoted it as being like a 'pen from another planet'.

The history of the often high-maintenance fountain pen speaks to how anachronistic it may seem in a digital age, and yet at the same time to how its nib and flowing ink lend weight, sensuousness, a sense of commitment and the personal touch to whatever is written with it. Personal, indeed, because over time the nib of a fountain pen actually shapes itself to reflect the pressure and angle of the user's grip – which is why the sharing of a fountain pen is typically discouraged by manufacturers. On the most refined pens the materials suggest the old-fashioned too: a barrel made of celluloid (which gives it a warmer handle), or an ink feeder made of the rubber and sulphur compound ebonite (which ensures the ink flows smoothly).

Opposite: Soviet leader Mikhail Gorbachev and US President Ronald Reagan signing the first treaty to eliminate nuclear missiles, in Washington in 1987.
Below: The Montblanc Meisterstück – for some, the most iconic of fountain pens.

The basic notion of a fountain pen dates to Roman times, when a hollow marsh grass stem would be cut at one end to create a nib and then filled with ink to feed it. Later, the caliph of Egypt is said to have demanded the devising of a reservoir-based pen in AD 953. In 1636 German inventor Daniel Schwenter first prototyped a more workable notion of a pen that carried its own ink supply, by setting a quill inside another quill and sealing the end with cork (Germans would also later pioneer the development of such advances as iridium-tipped nibs, to counter the softness of gold and the corrosive impact of ink on steel; and rubber that did not turn brittle as it aged). Over the following centuries versions of the fountain pen would be suggested by M. Bion in 1702, Peregrin Williamson in 1809, John Scheffer in 1819, and John Jacob Parker, who designed a self-filling pen in 1831. But it was the American Lewis Waterman's 1884 model that is considered to be the first practical fountain pen.

Waterman had the idea of placing an air hole in the nib and supplying ink to that through a grooved feed mechanism, which in turn was held by a barrel, which itself doubled up as a carrier for an ink reservoir. Among the many variants on some kind of external button by which to deflate and refill the reservoir, Walter Sheaffer – another major name in pen manufacturing – had huge success with his introduction of the widely copied lever filler in 1912. Little else would change until the early 1950s, with the widespread advent of the disposable ink cartridge, in glass and then in plastic – an idea that had first been patented, though never made, by Romanian inventor Petrache Poenaru as long before as 1827.

By the 1950s the fountain pen had become a mass-market object. With the inexorable rise of the ballpoint pen it was gradually overtaken in popularity, yet paradoxically, the very ubiquity of the ballpoint has contributed to the fountain pen's regaining an air of sophistication. It still has power – which is perhaps why Sylvester Stallone has recently had a signature fountain pen bespoke-made by the Italian artisanal firm Montegrappa.

Opposite: German writer Stephan Andres at his home in Positano, Italy, 1949.
Below: Australian aviator and inventor – and the first man to fly solo from England to Australia – Bert Hinkler with fountain pen in hand, 1928.

THE POCKET KNIFE

The maker of the Swiss Army knife, Victorinox, knows how practical its pocket tool can be: it has received countless tales of close-run escapes thanks to some or other blade on one of its products. It is why its models have been the standard-issue pocket knife to armed forces around the world since 1945 (it was actually American soldiers who first dubbed it the 'Swiss Army knife', after struggling to pronounce its name in German, *Offiziersmesser*), including to the tiny Swiss standing army, which it has supplied since 1891. That is just seven years after the company was founded by Karl Elsener in Ibach, Switzerland. Even NASA astronauts carry one. But, the maker adds, there is another reason for the family firm's success: even today receiving one's first pocket knife is a rite of passage for many a boy.

The first pocket knives have been dated to the late Iron Age, and were used through the centuries but were not widely affordable until the seventeenth century. Around 1650 the cutlery industry of Sheffield, England, began to make what were then known as 'spring knives' – because the blade clicked open or shut thanks to a spring along the back of the case – and it was soon taken for granted that a man would carry one about his person. Different cultures around the world developed their own classic versions of the pocket knife, from the French Opinel and Laguiole brands to the Japanese Higo no Kami, and from the American manufacturer Buck, whose knives were so ubiquitous that the 'buck knife' became a generic term, through to the many traditionally made in Solingen, Germany.

A pocket knife – which historically did not lock and so was largely ineffective as a weapon – was simply a handy tool for everyday tasks, be it cutting fruit or sharpening a quill (hence 'penknife'). Indeed, leading makers of the eighteenth century, such as George Wostenholm, George Ibberson and Joseph Rodgers, were soon equipping their products – forerunners of the Swiss Army knife – with tools for all kinds of purpose, including saws, corkscrews and something to remove stones from horses' hooves. Following the advent of tinned foods,

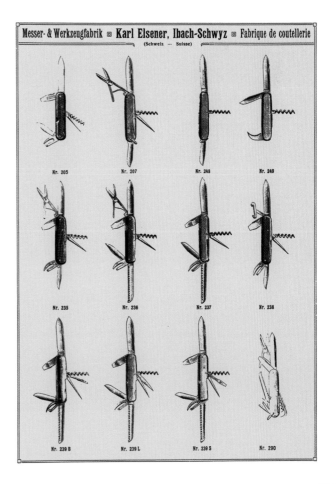

Opposite: Elvis Presley pointing a switchblade knife in a publicity still for his early acting career.
Right: A page from the 1903 Victorinox catalogue.

knives designed for soldiers, produced from the mid-nineteenth century, typically came with a tin opener too (tined foods allowed infantry to advance over longer distances without requiring supply chains of fresh produce).

Although such pocket knives were at least not initially considered to be weapons – in World War II, for example, Allied prisoners of war were typically allowed to keep theirs – pocket knives carried by sailors of the nineteenth century were said to be rounded off at the tip to minimize their effectiveness when stabbing. Perhaps the delinquents depicted in such movies as *Blackboard Jungle* (1955) and *West Side Story* (1961) were equally not to be trusted.

Utility was, after all, not the only thing that mattered about a man's pocket knife: its quality was something to display. It took master cutlers such as Ibberson to introduce knives with exotic handles made of pearl, ivory or tortoiseshell. Even stainless steel – said to have first been developed by Harry Brearley of Sheffield's Brown Frith Laboratories in 1913 – was initially prized as much for allowing a blade to retain its attractive polish as for preventing it from rusting. Certain individual makers had particular cachet: Ibberson's 'Stradivarius violin' trademark and 'Doublesharp' name, and Wostenholm's 'I*XL' trademark (still found on the British Army Knife) – became legendary markers on the best blades.

The Barlow knife, a historically favoured pocket knife style in the United States, distinctive for its one or two blades, outsize bolster (metal part joining the blade and handle) and teardrop-shaped handle, was first made in Sheffield, by Obadiah Barlow, around 1670. It too could cause boyish delight on being received as a present, as Mark Twain evoked so well in *The Adventures of Tom Sawyer* (1876): 'Mary gave him a bran-new "Barlow" knife worth twelve and a half cents; and the convulsion of delight that swept his system shook him to his foundations. True, the knife would not cut anything, but it was a "sure-enough" Barlow and there was inconceivable grandeur in that...'

Below: British athlete and explorer Chris Brasher uses his penknife to cut up dried, salted fish while on a 1958 expedition to scale Jangi-Tau in the Caucasus mountains. Opposite: Penknives from the traditional maker Taylor's Eye Witness, made in the heart of Britain's steel industry, Sheffield.

SUNGLASSES

If sunglasses are nowadays associated as much with projecting an image as protecting the eyes, that has not always been the case. In 1752 one James Ayscough began experimenting with blue- and green-tinted lenses in spectacles in the belief that they could correct eyesight impairments. Shielding the eyes from the sun was not then of concern, although in the nineteenth and early twentieth centuries, yellow-tinted glasses were prescribed to those suffering from syphilis, one of the symptoms of which is a sensitivity to bright light. The Chinese, however, as far back as the fourteenth century, understood that sunglasses' utility could be far more psychological than practical: judges wore glasses tinted with a smoky quartz to create an air of cool inscrutability and prevent onlookers from reading signs in their eyes. It was an idea that would catch on, albeit some 600 years later.

Indeed, while Hollywood stars of the early twentieth century were among the first to use sunglasses – initially as a means of protecting their eyes against the glare of studio lights between shots, and soon finding that it helped to protect them from unwanted attention – it would not be until 1929 that the first mass-manufactured sunglasses became commercially available. They were designed and made in Atlantic City, New Jersey, by Sam Foster and sold under the Foster Grant name as a means of protection from ultraviolet light.

But what really boosted public awareness of sunglasses was their take-up by the military and subsequent commercialization. The same year that Foster launched his model, Lieutenant-General MacCready of the US Army Air Corps commissioned the design of a pair of what were dubbed 'goggles' to give pilots a clear field of vision and help them cope with the intense, headache-inducing glare of the sun while flying above the clouds. In 1935 Bausch & Lomb put its model, the Type D-1, into production. The company would come to be internationally known as Ray-Ban the following year, when its D-1 model was launched to the public and was quickly picked up by keen sportsmen. That model – using a Polaroid filter patented for sunglasses by Edwin Land the same year – became better known as the Aviator.

Opposite: Tom Cruise feels the need for speed, and a pair of Ray-Ban Aviators, in *Top Gun* (1986).
Below: Jack Nicholson celebrates winning an Academy Award for Best Actor for his part in *One Flew Over the Cuckoo's Nest* in 1975.

The model resulting from the commission came with a plastic frame, so that no metal would touch the skin of ground-crew members working in sub-zero conditions (it was later replaced by a thin metal frame), and an anti-glare lens in a distinctive green colour (discovered to best absorb light in the yellow band of the spectrum). The lenses had a characteristic oversized teardrop shape, much the same shape as the goggles already in service. Thanks to the lenses coming low over the cheek to fully protect the entire eye socket, they left pilots with what was dubbed a 'Ray-Ban tan'. The style came to be embraced by naval flyers especially and even came to be a mark of distinctiveness; US Army and Air Force pilots typically preferred a smaller, squarer style by American Optical that became available in 1958 and could be easily removed or put on while wearing a helmet.

By the 1950s, the appeal of sunglasses as a means of creating an air of aloofness – if the eyes are the windows of the soul, then sunglasses are the shutters – was fast overtaking their protective value. In 1952, Ray-Ban launched perhaps its second most well-known style – and second most imitated – the Wayfarer. Smart technology played a part in its creation too: it was made from fully injection-moulded acetate. But what made it work commercially was that it had a simple shape with unisex appeal. The classic style became a cult thanks to its adoption by numerous icons of cool, including Bob Dylan and, later, Jack Nicholson.

Indeed, if the Aviator's purist design and functional style was underlined by its association in the movies with motorbike-riding and flying – from *Easy Rider* (1969) to, most famously, *Top Gun* (1986) – the chic of the Wayfarer and similar models was emphasized by its association with characters wearing them more for the sake of style: from Cary Grant in *North by Northwest* (1959) to Steve McQueen in *The Thomas Crowne Affair* (1968), from Clint Eastwood in *Dirty Harry* (1971) to (perhaps most famously of all) John Belushi and Dan Aykroyd in *The Blues Brothers* (1980). In real life, male celebrities ranging from Alain Delon to John Lennon in some part have often defined their public image by their attachment to sunglasses too.

Below: A Brooklyn gang on the boardwalk, Coney Island, in 1959.
Opposite: Yasser Arafat, leader of the Palestinian Fatah group, during a press conference in 1970.

THE UMBRELLA

When James Smith and Sons opened for business in London in 1830, it was the first shop to specialize in selling umbrellas. That it had taken so long for such a shop to open is at first surprising, given the fact that the device – first for providing shade, later for protection from inclement weather – had been around since perhaps the eleventh century BC, and was in use in the ancient civilizations of India, Greece, Egypt and China, among others. For many of these it was closely linked to social rank, especially since this was associated with fair skin, and it was sometimes part of ceremonial regalia. The Chinese were probably the first to waterproof a parasol against a downpour, its most common use today – even if 'umbrella' takes its name from the Latin *umbra*, meaning 'shade', which speaks to the device's origin as a means of keeping the sun off one's head.

From the sixteenth century, when some version of the device was first used in the West, until the early nineteenth century, the parasol had been pre-eminent. And the parasol was regarded as being strictly part of the female wardrobe. Indeed, when during the first half of the eighteenth century, the English traveller, philanthropist and writer Jonas Hanway made a habit of carrying an umbrella with him in public – as something of a style signature – it was initially considered a frivolous object, ungentlemanly, if not an outright affectation.

Yet throughout the middle decades of the eighteenth century, its practicality soon trumped any outdated ideas of propriety, especially in those climates where rain was commonplace and waterproofed clothing yet to be invented. Hanway is said to have become something of a hate figure for coachmen, who worried that this exotic, suspiciously foreign device's wider uptake would ruin their trade. A footman by the name of John MacDonald recalled in his 1750 memoir how he was shouted at on going out with his silk umbrella: 'Frenchman, why don't you get a coach?' But such was Hanway's influence that for some time the umbrella was referred to by his name. Tellingly, the first patent registered for an umbrella – as a canopy supported by ribbing from a central shaft – was not until 1786, the year of Hanway's death.

The umbrella soon became an accessory that was at once an intriguing piece of engineering – always evolving, becoming sturdier and lighter (a man's umbrella of the period could weigh up to 1.8 kilos [4 pounds]) – and an expression of some artistry. Early umbrellas comprised a wood or whalebone structure covered with oiled canvas, with 1843 seeing London gunsmith Henry Holland, inspired by the rising cost of whalebone, introduce the idea of using steel ribs. This idea was perfected in 1852 by one Samuel Fox, who would also establish one of Britain's pre-eminent makers.

Meanwhile, umbrellas were being prized – and shown off – for the sculptural qualities of their handles, carved in ebony or other hard woods. This gave the device some style when not in use. Carrying an umbrella might be said to have become a contemporary alternative to carrying a sword, as all gentlemen once did: it was something to brandish, point with or simply gleefully twirl, something maybe never even unfurled.

It is perhaps this that lent the tightly closed black umbrella – full-length, as opposed to the folding and telescopic variety that had been created in the United States during the 1930s – the characteristic of being somewhat dandyish. As stiffly uniformed as the mid-twentieth century's stereotypical City gent may have been, in his unwavering pin-striped suit and bowler hat, his carrying of an umbrella represented a touch of flamboyance – a fact played on during the 1960s by the actor Patrick Macnee as John Steed in the British television spy series *The Avengers*. The umbrella played its part in a real-life spy drama too: Bulgarian dissident Georgi Markov is believed to have been murdered in 1978 by way of a tiny pellet containing the toxin ricin being fired into his leg from the tip of a specially adapted umbrella as he was walking across London's Waterloo Bridge.

Opposite: Gene Kelly in a publicity image for *Singin' in the Rain* (1952).
Below: Patrick Macnee as John Steed, with signature bowler and brolly, in the 1960s British thriller series *The Avengers*.

SPECTACLES

'Film stars to me were always six feet four, had perfect teeth, could do handstands on Malibu beach – and didn't need glasses,' actor Michael Caine once said; his own heavy black frames were immortalized in photographer David Bailey's 1960s portrait of Caine. Certainly a latent negativity about glasses remains, so much so that it is said that an American presidential candidate will still lose crucial electioneering points for daring to express a frailty so blatantly. And yet towards the end of the twentieth century one study had it that almost one in ten sales of specs was to people with perfect eyesight, so deeply rooted is their evocation of intellectualism, or perhaps of the nerdiness of the late Steve Jobs or Bill Gates, respective founders of Apple and Microsoft. Such are spectacles' suggestion of braininess, rather than merely poor eyesight, that Cambodian dictator Pol Pot regarded them as a benchmark of potential dissidence. To wear glasses was to risk execution: short-sightedness suggested far too much reading.

It was not only for Michael Caine that glasses had become a form of distinctive sartorial signature: silent movie era superstar Harold Lloyd wore tortoiseshell specs, starting something of a craze. Buddy Holly reluctantly played against pop star stereotype, stumbling through many early performances in a blur until his supposedly 20/800 vision forced him to consent to wearing glasses, only to find they made him more, not less memorable. Many others followed his example, including musicians Hank Marvin, John Lennon, Elvis Costello and Elton John; cinema stars such as Peter Sellers and Woody Allen; and artist David Hockney, fashion designer Yves Saint Laurent and architect Le Corbusier. Mohandas Gandhi became recognized globally less for his clothing (he rejected Western dress in favour of the traditional hand-spun dhoti cloth) as for his round, metal-framed bifocals, which he once quipped gave him 'the vision to free India'.

In fiction, glasses can symbolize an alter ego and also play on the idea that they hint at a lack of manliness. Clark Kent wears frames as part of his disguise – until he becomes Superman, when, of course, he no longer requires them.

Opposite: Michael Caine in 1966, wearing the heavy-framed black glasses that would become a signature for him during the decade.
Below: Christopher Reeve as the bespectacled Clark Kent in *Superman* (1978), here with Margot Kidder.

'Look, they're all wearing glasses!' Jean Simmons exclaims in *The Grass is Greener* (1960), in which middle-aged men Cary Grant, Robert Mitchum and Moray Watson all must don specs in order to conduct a duel. Michael Caine used heavy Curry & Paxton glasses specifically to set his *Ipcress File* (1965) spy character Harry Palmer in opposition to the high glamour of the cinematic James Bond. Not that it stops Palmer from getting the ladies. 'Do you ever take your glasses off?' asks a woman for whom Palmer has just cooked a meal at his flat. 'Only in bed', he replies. Slowly, she removes his glasses. Fade to black…

Of course, glasses came about precisely because they did correct a frailty, not because they projected an image. In Europe they were first produced by an Italian in the late thirteenth century, although the English Franciscan philosopher and scientist Roger Bacon outlined the principles of corrective lenses in his *Opus Majus* of 1266. While historical records are imprecise, the earliest depiction of specs in a work of art can be dated precisely to 1352, in a series of frescoes by Tommaso da Modena for a basilica in Treviso, near Venice – and within a couple of decades Saint Paul was even being depicted wearing tinted specs in order to cope with the light of revelation.

But it was actually the invention of the printing press in 1452, and the accompanying boom in literacy and in inexpensive material to read, that encouraged the development and wider uptake of eyeglasses. Their evolution was slow, however. Temple pieces that sat over the ears so glasses did not have to be held in front of the face were not introduced until around 1728. Later would come specs with extra-long temples, all the better to wear with one's wig, while the 1840s saw a fashion once again for the temple-less style, so-called pince-nez, or 'pinch nose', coming out of France but finding popularity in the United States, where presidents Teddy Roosevelt and Calvin Coolidge were fans. Bifocals, enabling the use of two strengths of magnification in the same lens, were invented by Benjamin Franklin in 1784. Once his reading glasses were on, he is said to have disliked the inconvenience of having to take them off to look further afield.

Opposite: John Lennon in his round spectacles, with Yoko Ono, 1970s.
Below left: Woody Allen at home – his glasses underline his nebbish, nerdy image.
Below right: Buddy Holly performed in a blur for years before his manager persuaded him, rightly, that his distinctive glasses would prove a boon to his public image.

INDEX

Page numbers in *italics* indicate illustrations

PICTURE CREDITS

2 John Dominis/The LIFE Picture Collection/Getty Images; 7 Magnum Collection/Magnum Photos; 8 John Kobal Foundation/Getty Images; 10 Archive Images/Getty Images; 12 REX/Moviestore Collection; 13 (top) Chippewa Boot Company; 13 (bottom) REX/Moviestore Collection; 14 Rex; 15 Silver Screen Collection/Getty Images; 16 Terry O'Neill/Getty Images; 17 (left) Justin Boot Company 18 (right) Walter Sanders/The LIFE Picture Collection/Getty Images 18 Tony Lama Boot Company; 19 Burt Glinn/Magnum Photos; 20 (top) Museum of London/Heritage Images/Getty Images; 20 (bottom) Fine Art Images/Heritage Images/Getty Images; 21 Ferdinando Scianna/Magnum Photos; 22 (top) Michael Christopher Brown/Magnum Photos; 22 (bottom) Bettmann/CORBIS; 23 Dennis Stock/ Magnum Photos; 24 Michael Putland/ Getty Images; 26 SSPL/Getty; 27 (left) Brooks Brothers; 27 (right) REX/ Courtesy Everett Collection; 28 REX/ IPC MAGAZINES: CHAT; 29 Michael Ochs Archives/Getty Images; 30 Hulton Archive/Getty Images; 31 iStock; 32 MIRISCH-7 ARTS/UNITED ARTISTS / THE KOBAL COLLECTION; 33 Terry O'Neill/Getty Images 34 REPORTERS ASSOCIES/Gamma-Rapho via Getty Images 35 John Lobb 35 REX/Richard Young 36 Culture Club/Getty Images; 37 John Rawlings/ Condé Nast Archive; 38 David Hurn/Magnum Photos; 39 John Lobb 40 LCDM Universal History Archive/Getty Images; 41 Andre De Dienes/Condé Nast Archive 42 Everett Collection/REX; 44 Kangol; 44 Barratts/S&G Barratts/EMPICS Archive; 45 Stanley Bielecki Movie Collection/Getty Images; 46 Henri Cartier-Bresson/Magnum Photos; 47 Ted Spiegel/CORBIS; 48 Terry O'Neill/ Getty Images; 49 Nedim Nazerali Photography/Bates Hats/bates-hats. com 50 REX/c.Col Pics/Everett; 51 Werner Bischof/Magnum Photos; 52 (left) REX/Moviestore Collection;

52 (right) Michael Ochs Archive/ Getty Images; 53 (top) John Kobal Foundation/Getty Images; 53 (bottom) John Springer Collection/CORBIS; 54 REX/Everett Collection; 56 REX/Andre Csillag; 57 (left) Edward S. Curtis/ Corbis; 57 (right) Chi Modu/Diverse Images/Corbis; 58 Jay Brooks/PYMCA/ REX; 59 REX/BRIAN RASIC; 59 Condé Nast Archive; 60 Joseph Scherschel/ The LIFE Picture Collection/Getty Images; 61 (left) Charles Gatewood/ The Image Works/Topfoto; 61 (right) IWM/Getty Images; 62 REX/Sam Shaw/ Shaw Family Archive; 63 Mark and Colleen Hayward/Redferns/Getty 64 Frank Scherschel/The LIFE Picture Collection/Getty Images 65 (left) REX/Courtesy Everett Collection; 65 (right) Emmets Field Flannels-Brian Terreson 66 (left) Neal Preston/Corbis; 66 (right) Tim Roney/Getty Images; 67 Bettmann/CORBIS; 68 (top) REX/ Normski/PYMCA; 68 (bottom) Dave Bartruff/Genesis Photos/Corbis; 69 Corbis; 70 (top) John Bulmer/Getty Images; 70 (bottom) Jamel Shabazz/ Getty Images; 71 Dennis Stock/ Magnum Photos; 72 Terry O'Neill/Getty Images; 73 (left) Bettmann/CORBIS; 73 (right) Popperfoto/Getty Images; 74 REX/Everett Collection; 75 Ernst Haas/Getty Images; 76 REX/SNAP; 78 Eliot Elisofon/The LIFE Picture Collection/Getty Images; 79 (left) REX/ Courtesy Everett Collection; 79 (right) REX/c.Everett Collection; 80 REX/c. Everett Collection; 81 (top) REX/c. Everett Collection; 81 (bottom) Dave Hogan/Hulton Archive/Getty Images; 82 Murray Close/Getty Images; 83 (left) Picture Post/Hulton Archive/Getty Images; 83 (right) Advertising Archives; 84 (top) Vittorio Zunino Celotto/ Getty Images; 84 (bottom) John Jonas Gruen/Getty Images; 85 Advertising Archives; 86 ClassicStock/Corbis; 87 (left) Stock Montage/Getty Images; 87 (right) Alfred Eisenstaedt/The LIFE Picture Collection/Getty Images; 88 REX/c.Everett Collection; 89 KMazur/

WireImage/Getty; **90** Rex; **91** REX/
Moviestore Collection; **92** REX/Sipa
Press; **93** REX/SNAP; **94** REX/Courtesy
Everett Collection; **95** REX/Ian Dickson;
96 Keystone-France/Gamma-Keystone
via Getty Images; **97** Terry O'Neill/Hulton
Archive/Getty Images; **98** REX/Heikki
Saukkomaa; **99** Michael Ochs Archive/
Getty Images; **100** Ray Fisher/The
LIFE Images Collection/Getty Images;
102 (left) Nedim Nazerali Photography/
Hilditch and Key/hilditchandkey.com;
102 (right) Brooks Kraft/Corbis; **103** Ian
Berry/Magnum Photos; **104** Rolex/Alain
Costa; **105** Peter Stackpole/The LIFE
Picture Collection/Getty Images **106**
Omega Watches **108** IWC Schaffhausen
109 Brietling 'Limited Edition Navitimer
01' (silver dial/brown leather strap) –
AB012312/G756 RRP £6280 **110
(top)** REUTERS/Russell Boyce /Corbis;
110 (bottom) REX/Courtesy Everett
Collection; **111** Nancy R. Schiff/Getty
Images; **112** REX/Moviestore Collection;
114 (top) Bill Amberg-billamberg.com
114 (bottom) Bettmann/Corbis; **115**
Rex; **116** SSPL/Getty Images; **117**
Getty Images; **118 (top)** E.O. Hoppe/
Hulton Archive/Getty Images; **118
(bottom)** Scheufler Collection/CORBIS;
119 LUCASFILM/20TH CENTURY FOX
/ THE KOBAL COLLECTION; **120** REX/
SNAP; **122 (top)** REX/Sonny Meddle;
122 (bottom) Picture Post/Hulton
Archive/Getty Images; **123** SSPL/Getty
Images; **124 (left)** REX/Universal History
Archive; **124 (right)** Philippe Halsman/
Magnum Photos; **125 (left)** Loomis
Dean/The LIFE Picture Collection/Getty
Images; **125 (right)** Patrick Zachmann/
Magnum Photos; **126** REX/SNAP; **127
(left)** Charles Gatewood; **127 (right)**
akg-images; **128** Mr Hartnett/PYMCA;
129 Kirstin Sinclair/FilmMagic/Getty
Images; **130** John Kobal Foundation/
Getty Images; **132** REX/c.20thC.Fox/
Everett; **133 (top)** Jay Paull/Getty
Images; **133 (bottom)** Gamma-**Keystone**
via Getty Images; **134** REX/Toni Tye /
PYMCA; **135** Philippe Halsman/Magnum
Photos; **136** Silver Screen Collection/

Archive Photos/Getty Images **137 (top)**
Silver Screen Collection/Getty Images;
137 (bottom) REX/Everett Collection;
138 John Kobal Foundation/Getty
Images; **139** Bruce Gilden/Magnum
Photos; **140 (left)** A. Jones/Express/
Getty Images; **140 (right)** REX/Courtesy
Everett Collection; **141** Everett
Collection/REX; **142 (left)** UNITED
ARTISTS / THE KOBAL COLLECTION;
142 (right) REX/Magic Car Pics; **143
(top)** REX/Derek Cattani; **143 (bottom)**
Rene Burri/Magnum Photos; **144 (top)**
Evans/Three Lions/Getty Images **144
(bottom)** Michael Ochs Archives/Getty
Images; **145** CBS Photo Archive/Getty
Images; **146 (top)** Hulton Archive/Getty
Images; **146 (bottom)** Advertising
Archives; **147** Lambert/Getty; **148**
REX/Courtesy Everett Collection; **150**
DON EMMERT/AFP/Getty Images; **151**
Montblanc; **152** Herbert List / Magnum
Photos; **153** Topical Press Agency/Getty
Images; **154** John Springer Collection/
CORBIS; **155** Victorinox AG; **156** Paul
Popper/Popperfoto/Getty Images; **157**
Taylors Eye Witness Ltd; **158** Paramount
Pictures/Sunset Boulevard/Corbis;
159 Bettmann/CORBIS; **160** Bruce
Davidson/Magnum Photos; **161** Bruno
Barbey/Magnum Photos; **162** REX/
Moviestore Collection; **163 (top)** Fox
Umbrellas Ltd-foxumbrellas.com **163
(bottom)** REX/Studiocanal Films; **164**
REX/Monty Fresco; **165** REX/Everett
Collection; **166** Bob Thomas/Getty
Images; **167 (left)** Nancy R. Schiff/
Getty Images; **167 (right)** Hulton
Archive/Getty Images